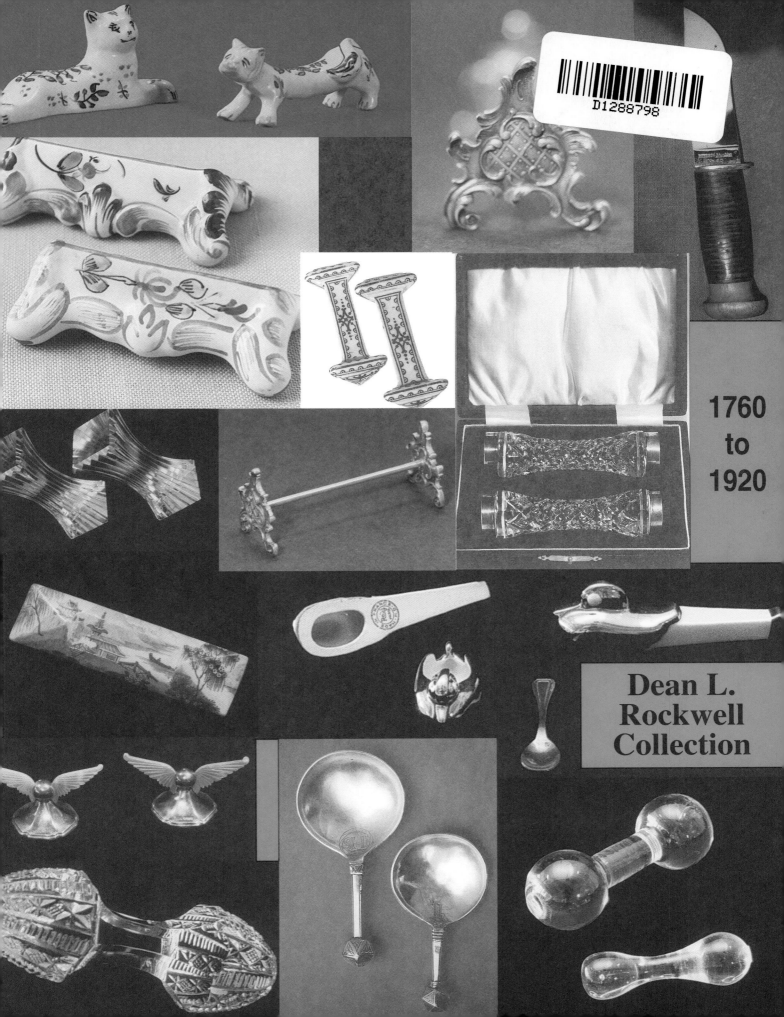

1760
to
1920

Dean L.
Rockwell
Collection

ANTIQUE KNIFE RESTS

The History, Manufacture and Use of English, American & Continental Knife Rests in Metal, Glass & Ceramic

By Dean Rockwell

Proctor Publications, LLC
Ann Arbor, Michigan, USA
www.proctorpublications.com

Proctor Publications, LLC
Ann Arbor, Michigan
Ypsilanti, Michigan
800-343-3034
www.proctorpublications.com

Publisher's Cataloging in Publication
(Provided by Quality Books, Inc.)

Rockwell, Dean
    Antique knife rests : history, manufacture, &
illustrations of American, English, & continental
knife rests in metal. glass, & ceramic / by Dean
Rockwell. -- 1st ed.
        p. cm.
        LCCN: 00-132734
        Includes bibliographical references.
        ISBN: 1-88279-295-5

    1. Knife rests--History. 2. Knife rests--
Collectors and collecting.   I. Title.

NK6150.R63 2000   642.7
                                            QBI00-476

Cover: English precelain knife rests probably *Minton*, c. 1850.
Beautifully painted birds. Rockwell collection.

Scotch Prayer

Some hae meat and cannot eat
Some can eat and hae no meat
We hae meat and we can eat
May the Lord be Thanket

Preface

My records show I purchased my first knife rest in 1968. The records also show my buying picked up steam as time went on. Well into my collecting career, as has happened with my acquisition of other art objects, i.e., the ceramic buying phase of my life, I realized I knew nothing about knife rests, their use, manufacture, history, types, or origin. I began to seek written information.

Imagine my surprise and modest disappointments when I found almost nothing about them. Questions to dealers and knowledgeable, long time collectors, and students, either drew blank stares or the reference to the same stale information that had been repeated for years.

So I said to myself, "Dean, there must be references to their origin and use somewhere. Get busy."

Spending days in libraries such as the Victoria and Albert and the British Museum in London, the Edward Drummond Libbey Library in Toledo, Ohio, the Robert H. Tannahill Library of the Henry Ford Museum in Dearborn, Michigan, and the Corning Museum of Glass, Corning, New York made for a lot of good reading, but only produced snippets of useful information. Most of the books and publications I read only referred to eating, manners, dining customs, and eating utensils.

My digging has paid off, for those snippets, recorded notes and other research, when put together have produced this book. 'Tis true it leaves many unanswered questions for later scholars, but perhaps this tome will fascinate you as my research did me while learning about their evolution, use, and contribution to the dining scene. Along the way I learned a lot of history, economics, customs, manners, and about human nature of peoples from ancient China, the near East, Greece, ancient Rome, medieval times, and today's societies. What have really changed are our eating habits, many of which I have chronicled here.

This monograph can't be the definitive work on knife rests; the field is too vast and unexplored. It will, I hope, leave much unanswered, and will motivate more, much more, study, research, and publishing. The newly organized *Knife Rest Collectors Society* will provide an excellent outlet for new findings.

My thanks again to the many courteous people in the libraries of my choice who were so helpful, and to all of you patient people who have lived long enough to see this book.

Dean Rockwell, B.S., M.A., F.R.S.A.

Acknowledgments

My study and research on knife rests covered some 25 years, mostly fits and starts, as I'd be motivated for a time, then another project would submerge knife rests and take precedence for awhile.

I did, however, in the time devoted, do considerable study at some prestigious libraries. I must commend the Victoria and Albert and the British Museum Libraries in London, England, the Edward Drummond Libbey Library in Toledo, Ohio, the City of Detroit Library, the Robert Tannahill Library of the Henry Ford Museum in Dearborn, Michigan, and the Corning Museum of Glass, Corning, New York for their help and courtesy. However, their many volumes related to dining contained almost nothing on the objects of my study.

Some people have been most helpful. Beverly Ales, a major collector, keen student, and publisher of the *Knife Rests of Yesterday and Today* in California, and Doreen Hornsblow of England, who publishes the *Knife Rest Collector's Club Newsletter* four times a year, have both been generous with permission to use some of their findings.

Some of the American metal knife rest manufacturers also made thimbles in the 19th and 20th centuries and a prominent Detroit thimble collector, Gloria Rousseaux, was most helpful in drawing my attention to the same factory marks on each item. For reference to French ceramics, I was able to use the extensive library of Don and Marilyn Ross.

I asked Renée Mitchell of Dearborn, Michigan to help me review and correct my grammar, sentence structure, and later to proof read the galley sheets. I didn't know what a treasure trove of knowledge, experience, and assistance I was getting. Renée, you have been invaluable to me and I thank you deeply.

No acknowledgment can be given without speaking of the late Sara Morse of New York and London, whose 2000 plus collection of knife rests, its displays, and news items provided the stimulus to many people to begin collecting these little gems.

Credit must also be given to Virginia L. Neas of Pickens, South Carolina, whose delightful book, *Knife Rests*, published in 1987, was the first and only book on these artifacts until now.

I wish to acknowledge the valuable help given me by the late Wilbur Pierce of Bloomfield Hills, Michigan, who gave me his considerable notes and research findings.

Table of Contents

ANTIQUE

KNIFE RESTS

The History, Manufacture and Use
of English, American & Continental
Knife Rests in Metal, Glass & Ceramic

Introduction

The origin, appearance, and use of the knife rests is not chronicled in dining and eating history as is the appearance of the knife, fork, spoon, and other dining tools and accoutrement.

They appeared on dining tables with the increased importance of fine dining during the early Georgian period in England. Despite being at war somewhere during all of this period, its prosperous times created a wealthy class which was able to copy the habits of nobility and the gentry.

Gone was the custom of eating with one's fingers from a common "mess". No longer did dinner guests have to bring their own cutlery, instead the host supplied a knife, fork, and spoon for each diner. They brought cleanliness and proper conduct to the table.

This also brought order to the dining scenes, manners to the diners, and lavish accoutrement to the table; including fine china, silver, eating utensils, candelabra, glass, crystal, and fine white tablecloths. And what hostess would not cringe to see a soiled knife, fork, or spoon laid upon her beautiful linen or damask tablecloth.

Guests at fine dinners were carefully selected and invited and only invited back if they passed the increasingly rigid rules of dining etiquette. Some of the rules were written; most were not. Who would dare place his dirty eating utensil on the fine linen; not if he wanted to receive another dinner invitation!

So, the stage was set for the appearance of some type of device on which to rest the used utensil. It had to evolve from some simple form, perhaps a piece of wood or bone fragment, surely not as displayed by the few delightful 18th century knife rests occasionally seen made of ceramics or sterling.

Lengthy and concentrated research of the written word has not disclosed any date nor reference to the appearance and use of the knife rest at any eating occasion, nor revealed to in the scores of books on dining and household management written during the Georgian and Victorian times. It is very possible knife rests originated on the Continent and spread to England. I've found nothing to support this, but it is just for more study.

Knife rests were only a minor manifestation of what was occurring in Georgian England;

elaborate meals, beautiful dining settings, changes in social mores and manners, both social and dining had to follow. *"Dinner parties rank first among all entertainment."*, wrote an anonymous member of the aristocracy in an English manners book dated 1779.

An invitation to dinner conveyed a greater mark of esteem than to any other gathering and, most importantly, is a civility that can be exchanged. Therefore, manners and politeness were given increasing importance. One of the purposes of the rise in table manners in the post medieval world, in both England and the Continent, was to prevent violence at or away from the table. Manners and politeness succeeded so well they eventually became ways of life in all strata of society. Manners at the table may be formally recognized, but it is the practice of informal manners that makes for pleasant social living.

I believe this book will show the knife rest as a dining device that was part of the increasing importance of manners and the formality of correct dining. There was a need for them, and they evolved as did the use of the fork and spoon, not really necessities until dining rituals became "musts".

It must be noted that uses of dining tools, manners, and more, like other social customs and practices, began with royalty, then downward to the nobility, gentry, and bourgeoisie, working their way down as fast as each level of society was ready and could afford them.

The popular use of the knife rest had begun to decline in the early 20th century and in the 1920s, right after World War I, the institution of live-in servants began to die out in North America and England (the process had already started in Europe).

Industrialization and its opportunities for paid work, with fixed hours and days off, sounded the death knell for the ready availability of a servant class. There would be no one to polish the silver. It would be lightly plated with non-tarnish chromium or platinum. Dishwashers and laundry machines would replace the washerwoman; soap powders and chemicals would do away with the necessity of sending soiled clothing out to be cleaned, and so forth.

While this book will refer repeatedly to dining, its customs and tools in Continental society, the thrust of this tome will be to the knife rest in England, America, and the English speaking world which evolved concurrently, but separately.

"If I should live to a ripe old age may I possess some bit of individuality, charm and wit. That I may not be discarded when I'm withered, worn and weak, but sought after and cherished like a fine antique."　　Author unknown

The Knife Rest

A little known or appreciated artifact that graced the Victorian English table, and was an essential part of any genteel dining table in our country during the Brilliant Period of glass, has become a much sought after collectors item. Even today, knife rests are a part of better dining in many Continental countries.

Made of glass, pressed or cut, metal, ceramic, bone, ivory, sometimes in combination with jade, marble, agate, horn, or tusk, and mother of pearl, these utilitarian devices show the imagination and skill of the designers and manufacturers, and the craft of the glass cutters. English knife rests reflect the life styles of over 200 years of the people and country, from simple Georgian design to rococo, baroque and Art Nouveau. Their use and popularity had reached their zenith by World War I after which the decline in the wide use of servants, the popularity of large formal dinners, the use of cut glass and a changing life style, signaled the end of their popular usage.

The evolution and use of eating utensils took many centuries.* Their use, as is customary today, is hardly 200 years old. The general availability and use of the knife, fork, and spoon at all meals in the latter half of the 18th century had a dramatic effect on dining in England. Until the middle of the 18th century, guests were expected to bring their own eating tools. With the advent of the Georgian Period (1760-1830) guests were no longer expected to supply their own cutlery.

Georgian dinner tables became works of art with silver, candelabra, linens, and lovely dinner services. Mahogany furniture, paintings on the walls, statuary, crystal, ceramic centerpieces called epergnes, intricate plaster designs on the walls and ceilings, all set off by wallpaper of exotic scenes often completed the setting.

Table accoutrement, to prevent soiling of the table linens, were certainly normal and necessary additions to the dining table. Therefore knife rests had to be invented – or devised. There does not seem to be any historical date of their

appearance on the social scene, but there are rests hallmarked in the late George III period and pottery rests certainly of late 18th century creamware. It remained for them to gain their greatest popularity during the reign of Queen Victoria (1837-1901). During her time on the throne, England enjoyed the longest reign of any of her monarchs, and an unprecedented period of peace, prosperity, and colonial expansion ruled. Her influence as an industrial, commercial, and so

Victorian dining table. Note the knife rests at either end.

cial leader was at its greatest.

This period saw an increasing wealthy class of industrialists, bankers, ship owners, publishers, shipping brokers, and politicians. Nobility and landed gentry, who could afford servants and a genteel life style, entertained lavishly with large, formal dinners complete with fine china, silver, crystal, and linen. It also set the style for a growing middle class.

Histories of dining and table manners do not tell us whether the knife rest was first used by each diner to protect the linen or whether they were immediately used as supports** for only the carving knife and forks.

Any large dinner or special occasion, especially on Sunday, could demand a "joint" (roast, usually of beef) which would be put at the head of the table to be carved by the host. The knife rests were set on each side of the platter so the carving knife and fork could be placed on them. This saved the table linen from being soiled when the knife and fork were not in use. The joint of beef might also be placed on a nearby sideboard and a pair of knife rests would be there also.

Occasionally another pair of knife rests would be found at the other end of the table to be used by the hostess, or someone so appointed, to do the carving of a different type of meat, or to be used after serving the dessert or sweet. In simpler settings the meat would be placed before the father, dinner plates on the left, knife rests on the right on which he'd place the utensils after they had b e e n wiped free of juice or gravy.

In the United States, as well as most English speaking countries, it is the custom, and mannerly, to p l a c e soiled eating utensils on ones plate or side dish. Logical deduction leads one to believe the use of knife rests in England, soon after their introduction, was related to meat carving only, while soiled eating cutlery was placed on the dinnerware to protect the linen.

Based on the dating of the manufacture of glass knife rests in this country, they did not become a prominent part of the dining scene until the Brilliant Period of cut glass (1880-1915). And as in England, they began to decline in usage after World War I for the same reason, i.e., fewer servants, less lavish entertaining, decline in the popularity of cut glass, and changing social customs. However, before the rise in popularity of cut glass, there is ample evidence of the popularity of metal knife rests, beginning about 1850.

But during the Brilliant Period glassmakers such as *Libbey, Hawkes,* and *Hoare* produced some of the finest examples of cut crystal knife rests to be seen anywhere. The quality of the crystal, the originality of design and the sharpness of the cuts were superb. Obviously, other glass companies produced rests during this period but many cannot definitely be ascribed

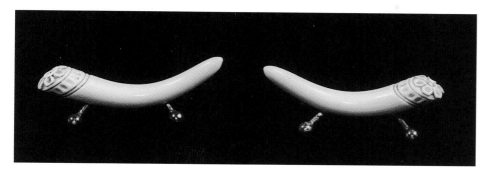

probably gold. The metal was cast, bent, and hammered into unique shapes sometimes rococo, and sometimes taking the shape of animals. One set in the author's possession, shows one athlete competing against another in different sports.

to any maker, 'tho many are of high quality and show great originality and fine workmanship.

Knife rests in England and the U. S. almost always were made and used in pairs, be they metal, glass, ceramic, or whatever. Not uncommonly those of metal would carry a family crest or initials. Occasionally they are found in satin or velvet lined cases of two or four, showing the care and pride bestowed upon them.

On the Continent, especially in France, where they are still a part of a proper meal in better homes, they are used by all the diners and are found in matching sets of up to 16 in number. Commonly used even today in the Scandinavian countries, some parts of Germany, Austria, and the Netherlands, they are not just for the carving set, but for each individual person who places the used utensil on the rest to prevent soiling the linen. In Holland today it is said that when a bride-to-be picks out her silver and china, she also chooses her knife rest pattern.

While glass or crystal was the most popular material for knife rests, metal ran a close second. In addition to those of sterling silver, in superb taste and design, they were made of silver and nickel plate on steel, Britannia metal, brass and white metal, pewter, plain brass, copper and

Whatever knife rests are made of, they can be classed as true art forms that reflect people's life styles, changing social customs, and eating habits, as well as demonstrating the imagination of the designers and the skills of artisans anywhere.

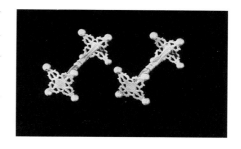

The Chinese claim to have used knives and forks about 4000 years ago but found them messy and gradually shifted to chopsticks.

Sometimes called "carving dogs" or "carvers rests".

Metal Knife Rests

While glass was the most popular medium for the manufacture of knife rests, metal really provided an opportunity for expression not possible in glass. In metal they have taken the form of birds, dogs, alligators, elephants, donkeys, chickens, cats, swans, squirrels, horses heads, and mythological beasts. Other designs were made in the form of flowers, buildings, cupids, athletes, and garden fences. These figures usually made up the end rest with the crossbar or support in between. The bodies of animals, such as dogs, foxes, etc., were often elongated with the feet as the end rest and the animal's back as the cross or support bar.

They are made of iron, brass, steel, silver, pewter, zinc, copper, Britannia metal, white metal, and, 'tho none have come to light, probably gold. And why not?

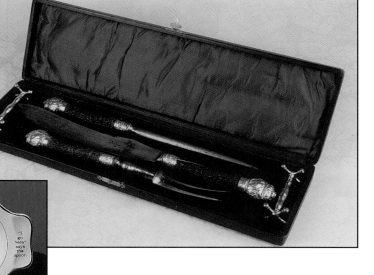

Metal can be formed by bending, stamping, casting, or hammering and be solid of one metal or more. Types of metal can be combined and all or part electroplated with silver, nickel, or gold.

In the United States, as well as in most English speaking countries, it is the custom and mannerly, to place soiled eating utensils on one's plate or side dish. As a consequence, there is no need for a knife rest at each place setting. Children were taught to place their knife and fork on the side of their child-plate. (See picture)

Metal knife rests in America tended to be much more exotic, or even bizarre, in design and shape than those from England or the Continent. Such companies as the *Meriden Britannia Company* of Meriden, Connecticut, were producing large quantities in metal, and their catalog of 1882 shows many with animal and human motifs. Metal rests are much more likely to be identifiable for the factory name was often part of the mold, or die, to appear raised or recessed on the finished rest.

During the latter part of the 19th century and into the 20th century, large dinner cutlery sets were popular and included knives, forks, and spoons for every course; soup, fish, entree, dessert, cheese, and coffee. Carving sets consisting of knife and fork are sometimes found with one or more pair of knife rests.

A few words about knife rests made of silver. When made of English *sterling*, 92.5% pure,

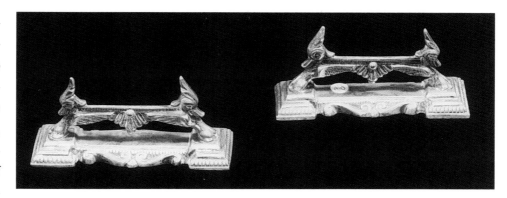

they were by law required to be hall-marked with a stamp showing the assay office, the year and the symbol for sterling, and usually, not always, the cipher of the silversmith. Frequently, one will find those stamped 975, 950, or even 925. This indicated the parts of silver per 1000, and are almost always Continental. However, some Continental ones will be stamped *sterling* as well. Silver rests made in the U. S. are usually stamped *sterling*

also. Any carrying the letters EPNS (electroplated nickel silver) are silver electroplated onto a base metal.

    Sterling silver shapes tend to be restrained

and dignified. Research shows that the earliest metal knife rests were probably made of pewter with silver to follow and crafted by some of the finest silversmiths. They were rarely used with ordinary dinner services, but because sterling has always been a symbol of elegance, refinement, and personal achievement, were reserved to be displayed with the fine china settings only.

Sterling knife rests continued to be made throughout some 140 years of popular use. Frequently, examples are found bearing family crests or initials, which only adds to their value and desirability as examples of an era of genteel dining now past.

    The author has never seen any made of so-called *Sheffield* silver plate, i.e., silver sheet laminated to base metal. It is logical to assume they were made to complement sets of *Sheffield* silver dinner service pieces.

Identifiable metal knife rests have been found from European companies in Sweden, Denmark, France, Germany, Austria, Hungary, and Russia.

Christofle of St. Denis, a suburb of Paris, produces fine metal knife rests even today. They are made in multiple sets, one for each dinner setting and are still in popular use in Europe.

Swedish knife rests tend to take simple shapes and are almost always metal. Their widespread use ended shortly after World War II and today are collectors items.

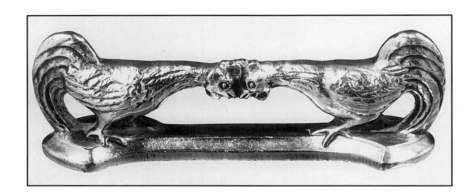

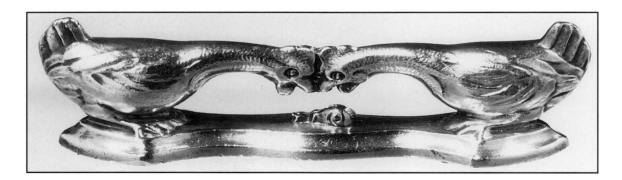

Ceramic Knife Rests

The term "ceramic" includes articles made of pottery or porcelain. Some of the finest knife rests were made of the potter's clay, and like metal, could be molded into charming and useful shapes. These took the form of fruit, flowers, and animals, such as seals, rabbits and elongated French grasshoppers.

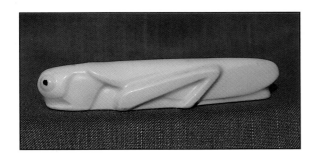

Perhaps it is time to note the difference between porcelain and pottery (earthenware). Porcelain was made of better material, e.g., china clay, china stone, calcined flint and, in the case of bone china, the addition of up to 50% calcined* ox bones ground to a powder. This gave the china added translucency, less likely to chip or crack and an excellent palette for the colors of the decorator. It was fired at high temperatures, almost as high as that needed to make glass.

Pottery, or earthenware, was made in many forms, e.g., stone china, redware, etc., using lesser grades of the above materials, excluding bone ash. By not firing at high temperatures and not as long in the kiln, pottery could be produced more cheaply than porcelain. But it provides some

excellent ware including creamware and pearlware of the 18th and 19th centuries that pro-

vided great opportunities for decorators. Decorating could be done either in colors or by transfer printing, especially the blue so well known in the willow patterns.

Earthenware is opaque. By holding a plate, or whatever, before a strong light, if you can see your fingers, it is porcelain; if not, it is pottery.

We'll turn first to England and the ceramic industry there. Many well known firms were producing knife rests early in the 19th century. Many are recognized names even today - *Davenport, Meir, Rogers, Spode, Minton, Leeds, Swansea,*

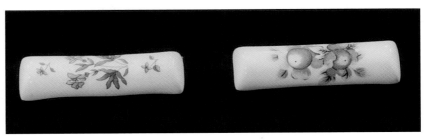

Creamware, *Wedgwood* - Rockwell collection

Wedgwood, Copeland Garrett, Clews, and *Derby.* Usually these were simple modified rectangular shapes, rounded on top but often with an indented center trough to catch the gravy running back down a carving knife. Often they were decorated in transfer patterns printed in color, frequently matching the pattern of the dinner set. They are very attractive bits, some hand decorated. Many are readily identifiable having the pottery company's name either back stamped in color, or impressed on the bottom. Some can also be identified with certain firms. Variations of chinoiserie patterns were frequently used; especially the willow pattern.

The number of potteries that went into business in the last half of the 18th century, and the volume of their productions, is a testimony to the greater prevalence and use of the knife, fork, and spoon for they required a hard surface to permit the diner to cut and manipulate his food. The potters can be thankful for this change in eating habits.

English ceramic knife rests can almost certainly be attributed to the first half of the 19th century and the last part of the 18th. The author has seen only one English knife rest in porcelain. Apparently, they were never used with fine bone china or porcelain dinner sets. Instead, they were

part of the popular transfer printed blue and white pottery dinner, supper, and dessert sets of this period. Fine china called for sterling silver, which

has always been a symbol of elegance, refinement, and personal achievement.

While the *Wedgwood Company*, founded by the great Josiah in 1759, did produce blue printed knife rests, usually marked on the bottom, they also made knife rests of famous Queensware** in at least three different shapes. Two of the three shapes were triangular with the crossbar of the third resting on three legs. While these three shapes are first seen in the factory shape book with the paper watermark of 1802, there is every reason to believe they were also made in the 18th century as well. They appear with other items manufactured much earlier than 1802. This supports the belief that ceramic knife rests had become part of the dining scene in the 18th century.

The author has never seen or found any knife rests of more than four in a set that had been part of dining in England, or in this country. Four in a set are very uncommon. They are usually in pairs, even those of the late 18th century, which supports the belief they were already in use then and used for the carving ceremony only.

While there are many examples of knife rests produced in America by the great glass manufacturers, there was, apparently, almost no production of ceramic knife rests by American potters. This can be attributed historically to the fact that the makers of fine china and pottery in this country did not come into their own until near the end of the 19th century. By the time the bride and the housewife recognized American quality, World War I was over and the popularity and use of knife rests had begun to decline. So, for perhaps a hundred years, pottery and porcelain knife rests had been imported from England and the Continent along with, or as a complement to, the dinnerware and fine china sets found in American homes.***

A reference in an early catalog of the *Dedham Pottery Company*, Dedham, Massachusetts, offers knife rests among other incidental pottery items.**** No examples have been seen by the author, 'tho a dealer has provided me with a photo of one.

Continental potters made their ware quite a bit more identifiable. Knife rests made by the French firm *Quimper****** usually have the name painted on by the decorator. They will have a round or triangular crossbar, connecting almost always with triangular end pieces. Their decorations are usually in red, green, blue, and yellow with the decorators letting his hand go free with stripes, bands, and swirls.

The famous *Meissen* porcelain factory in Germany is still producing these delightful and charming items, some in the form of simple bars, others in attractive geometric shapes, and still others with molded flowers or leaves attached. Earlier ones show the *Meissen* crossed swords mark, later ones may carry the name *Meissen*. All were made for individual use and must have added a colorful touch to the dining table. Another German ceramic knife rest firm, *Hutschenreuther* of Dresden, most likely of early 20th century manufacturing, has been identified.

The *Royal Copenhagen Porcelain* manufacturer of Denmark, founded in 1775, is still producing knife rests in simple but charming forms with traditional underglaze blue decoration. They can always be identified by the factory trademark of three wavy parallel blue lines back stamped on the bottom.

Other European potteries whose knife rests are collectible and readily identifiable by factory mark include *Sevres*, *Dresden*, *Limoges*, *Berlin*, *Baccarat*, and more.

While ceramic knife rests continue to be popular on the Continent right up to this day, their use in England began to decline late in the reign of Queen Victoria (1837-1901). Cut and pressed glass made by the renowned *Apsley Pellatt* of London and *Stourbridge* glassmakers, became the popular medium.

*Calcination materials such as coal (to coke), flint, ox bones, etc., are heated to high temperatures in the absence of oxygen, thereby driving off all volatile matter leaving only the solids.

**In 1759 Josiah Wedgwood I began the potting of his vastly improved creamware. After the acceptance by Queen Charlotte, in 1764, of a

breakfast service, he called the ware "Queensware."

***Only one ceramic knife rest made in this country can be reasonably identified with a specific company. The Brooklyn Museum, Brooklyn, New York, contains a pair of fine molded white porcelain knife rests identified as being produced by the Charles Cartlidge Co., Greenpoint, Long Island, New York. Cartlidge was born in the English potteries in 1800 and came to this country in 1832. He started his own pottery in 1848. It closed in 1856.

****My thanks to Bea Cohen of Easton, PA for the photos and for bringing Dedham to my attention.

*****When the Faienceries de Quimper, H. B. Henroit went bankrupt in 1983, the factory was purchased by the Americans, Mr. & Mrs. Paul Jannssens', thereby saving a pottery that had been (and still is) in continuous operation for over 300 years.

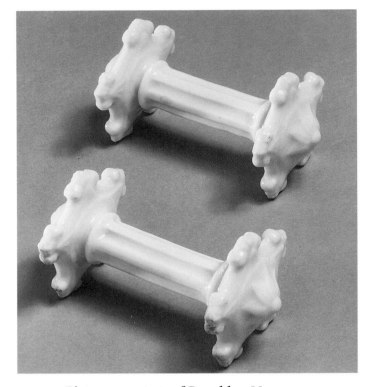

Picture courtesy of Brooklyn Museum

Glass Knife Rests

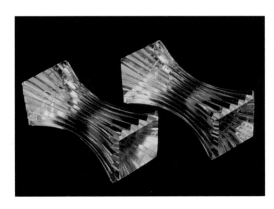

Glass was the single most popular material for knife rests. The quality ranged from the very ordinary, used in cheap pressed glass that sold for ten cents apiece, to the fine leaded crystal made by *Libbey, Hawkes,* or *Hoare* in the U. S., which now command premium prices to collectors.

While clear glass or crystal was used the most, many were made of colored glass, usually pressed, but sometimes in a combination of cut and molded. They were made in delicate shades of green, rosy pink, wine red, several shades of blue, an almost black purple, yellow, and smoky topaz. There are rare examples of vaseline and milk glass, and a frosted glass (usually *Lalique*).

Generally, all glass knife rests are of the dumbbell shape, almost always so if they are cut glass. The basic shape is made by the glass blower, then shaped on the cutter's wheel to the desired pattern. The crossbar is usually cut with six, sometimes four, and rarely eight surfaces. It may be round or with a cut design that is an integral part

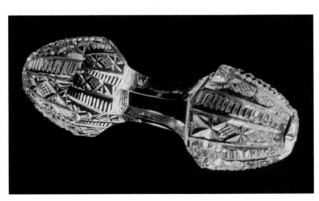

of the patterns on the ends. The end balls may not be necessarily round, but may be oval, square, triangular, elongated, or have a flat edge to prevent rolling.

Pressed glass knife rests were cast in molds and frequently in shapes other than round, especially so if they are made to include an open salt. One very unusual one in the author's collection has a 1" bar on either side which are inclined gently to the round salt in the center (overall length 3-3/4") to prevent utensils slipping off and soiling the tablecloth. This, of course, was for an individual setting and possibly for the eating knife on one side, fork on the other. It is impressed - Combination Pat., February 27, 1872.

Occasionally one finds other "double" knife rests in cut glass that will hold both knife and fork. The range in sizes suggests the large ones were for carving and the smaller ones for individual use. Could there have been periods and/or areas in this country where there was a knife rest for each diner? This possibility is an area open for study and research by collectors and students of early American dining.

Sizes of glass knife rests vary from six and one-half inches in length, with end balls of up to two and one-half inches in height, to "babies" of three inches long and barely one-half inch high.

The designers and cutters were fairly limited as to shapes, but when it came to patterns and designs, their imaginations and skills seemed limitless. More knife rests appear with the so-called "lapidary cut" but since they were often made to match or complement a crystal service, their patterns would be the same. However, many of the larger glass manufacturers, particularly in the U. S., offered only certain standard cut rests in their catalogs. Whether that was a "take these or else" situation, we do not know. But the wide variety of designs and cuts that show up in any sizeable collection of these art forms can only suggest that one could easily have had knife rests cut to taste. A much wider choice of designs was offered by such as *Libbey* in their catalogs of 1896, 1902, 1906, and 1908.

When made of leaded crystal and cut sharply with flutes, ribs, diamonds, facets, and swirls, they will shine and sparkle with the brilliance of gems.

Generally glass knife rests were made in England and the U.S. in pairs for the carving ceremony. On the Continent, especially in France, each guest had a knife rest, which was used to rest their soiled knife or fork. These knife rests were of a much simpler shape and design, usually square, flat, or three sided, sometimes cut glass, sometimes of metal, but always of high quality. The author has sets of eight, twelve, and sixteen; many boxed in fitted cases.

Lapidary cut

Identification of glass knife rests is very difficult, unless they carry an etched maker's mark or can be definitely identified in a manufacturers sales catalog. As an example, knife rests with the lapidary cut (the most popular) were produced by many manufacturers in nearly the same configuration, and appear in the sales catalogs of *Libbey, Mt. Washington Glass Co., Sinclaire,* and others. The only signed ones we have seen are *Libbey, Hawkes,* or *Hoare.*

Several theories for this oversight may come to mind. Knife rests were of so minor a value that the cost of etching was not economical. They were too unimportant a part of a service or of production to warrant signing, or, the blanks were made by a few glassmakers and then sold or sent to cutters or wholesalers for cutting, thereby making etching unlikely.

We have seen no signed knife rests that were made by English glassmakers. There is an example in the museum of the *Stevens and Williams Glass Co., Ltd.,* Brierley, Staffordshire, England. It is of good quality, but not signed or distinctive enough to serve

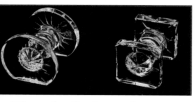

as a guide to identification of others. Glass knife rests are

Waterford: **pictured are two of the knife rests made there late in the 20th century. Both shapes were apparently being produced until 1993 when manufacture of the large square one ceased. The round one, in several designs is still being made.**

often found in combination with plated metal or sterling, which is usually hallmarked; these knife rests are almost certainly English glass.

Yet, the sheer quantity and quality of cut glass knife rests available to the collector in the United Kingdom is an indication of the volume

surely to have been made by English glassmakers or imported. This shows the popularity of the knife rest, especially during the Victorian Period (1837-1901) when gracious dining became the norm. In the Stourbridge and Birmingham districts alone, in 1841, there were 22 glass cutting establishments, apart from the manufacturers doing engraving themselves. The *Waterford Crystal Glass Co.*, of Ireland, is still making knife rests; these are signed by etching.

Apsley Pellatt (1791-1863), celebrated London glassmaker, was granted a patent in 1819 for a process of glass incrustation which he called "Crystallo Ceramic". Collectors usually refer to them as "sulfides", encrusted glass, or crystal cameos. By this process, knife rests could be embellished, though their 1840 catalog shows no knife rests. However, the great collection of the late Sara Moss did contain some.

The Continental glass knife rest usually found by collectors today are *Sèvres, Daum, St. Louis, Baccarat, Lalique,* and *Sabino*, all French.

All are usually signed and the latter three are still being made today. The *Sèvres, St. Louis,* and *Baccarat* marks will be acid etched while *Lalique* and *Sabino* marks take the form of engraved signatures. *Lalique* is further identified by their use of frosted glass, often with the bust of a cupid on either end of the crossbar. The collector should beware of those pieces that are frosted but not signed. The *Val St. Lambert Co.* of Belgium produced some rather simple pressed glass knife rests with a ground flat on either end.

As indicated elsewhere, the only positively identifiable American glass knife rests we have seen are those by the *Libbey Glass Co.*, Toledo, Ohio; the *T. G. Hawkes Glass Co.*, Corning, New York; *Hoare & Co.*, Corning, New York, and the *Heisey Glass Co.*, Cambridge, Ohio. The first three have acid etched signatures and all are of superb quality and cut. Careful examination is needed to find the marks. The word *Libbey* surmounts their Toledo sword trademark and is usually close to the shoulder of the end ball on one of the flats. The *Hoare* etching is usually on the center of one of the flats and takes the form of *J. Hoare*

& Co., in a circle, in the center of which is the year 1853. The *Hawkes* knife rest carries the plain etched signature *HAWKES* close to a shoulder either parallel or perpendicular on the flat. Holding the knife rest directly in front of a strong light

and rotating it slowly, allowing the light to shine through, has been found to be the best way to locate a mark.

Other American glassmakers whose records show they made knife rests include the 1874 catalog of the *Boston & Sandwich Glass Co.*, Boston, Massachusetts; the 1884 catalog of the *New England Glass Works*, Boston, Massachusetts (later moved to Toledo, Ohio to become the famed *Libbey Glass Co.)*; *Sinclaire*; the *Westmoreland Glass Co.*, Grapeville, Pennsylvania (made a pressed glass knife rest in 1900 that sold for ten cents); and an early *Mt. Washington Glass Co.*, New Bedford, Massachusetts catalog showing three standard patterns. About 1875 *Hartell & Letchworth*, glass manufacturers of Philadelphia, Pennsylvania, were producing pressed glass knife rests. No examples of this company's work is known.

The *Heisey Glass Co.* made pressed glass knife rests apparently right up until they were acquired by the *Imperial Glass Co.*, and these can be identified readily by the raised diamond with the H in the center. The *Cambridge Glass Co.*, Cambridge, Ohio, made pressed glass knife rests until acquired also by *Imperial*. As late as 1965, *Imperial,* Bellaire, Ohio was making pressed glass knife rests, and for a short time, about 1950, the same mold was used to produce knife rests in milk glass.

The Knife

Knife on left is copper, c. 3000 BC others are flint, Denmark, c. 3000 BC.

Certainly the knife, in some form, was a tool or implement carried by most men since the use of metal began. They served for offense, defense, and eating. Food in ancient, medieval, and well into the middle ages, usually took two forms: either a soupy, mushy like conglomerate called a "mess" eaten by scooping it up with your hand or a piece of bread from a common dish, or a haunch or loin of meat from which all diners carved slices with his knife, to be picked up with the fingers or speared and conveyed to one's mouth. The knife became the tool to cut, spear, and convey, 'til the popular use of the fork.

Prehistoric man used knives mostly made of flint, stone, slate, or obsidian. Later man could have used bone, wood, or shell for scraping, cutting, or possibly defense or combat.

The knife could be useful for splitting firewood, scaling fish, slicing vegetables, mincing meat, crushing garlic, cutting one's nail, and sharpening pencils. It could also be used for whittling, killing pigs, shaving (if kept sharp enough), settling old or new scores with enemies - AND for eating.

At first and for many centuries, there was no difference between the knife a man hunted with, fought with, or ate with. Until the 17th century at least, it was customary for each man to help himself at every meal with his own knife.

Eating tools were extremely personal possessions and were carried as necessities. Hosts, inns, and hostelries only furnished food and dining utensils; usually wood or pewter.

The "Bronze Age", (c. 3500 B. C.): Bronze was copper with a 10% alloy of tin and which could be sharpened to make knives. The "Iron Age", (c. 1100 B. C.) followed during which iron gradually replaced bronze.

Iron found its way to Britain around the middle of the 1st century B. C.. Julius Caesar noted its use there at the time of his 55 and 54 B. C. visits. The Romans were very adept at fashioning cutting instruments and brought with them specialized knives for a variety of purposes, including eating. Their forged shapes of iron tools for cutting, butchering, pruning, and harvesting were much the same as they are today.

In Saxon England during the 5th to 11th centuries the knife, called the "scramasax", never left its owner day or night, and was more in the nature of a dagger used for defense and combat as well as eating. It often carried the name of the owner along with a brief grace inlaid or engraved on the handle, to be said before meals.

As early as the 14th century there are references to sets of knives being provided by the host for his guests. But the practice of providing full place settings for each guest is, however, comparatively recent; probably in the latter half of the 18th century. With the place settings came crystal, fine dinnerware, snow-white linens, candelabra, AND table manners.

A 15th century writer offered some sound advice on behavior at the table. "It is wrong to grasp food with both hands at once. Meat should be taken with three fingers and too much should not be put into the mouth at one time. People should not scratch themselves at meals and then put their fingers in the food."

During the Middle Ages, Toledo, in Spain, and Damascus, in Syria were renowned for their cutlery, especially swords. England's Sheffield was known for the excellency of its knives as early as the reign of Richard I (1189-1199).

Knives in the traditional view are "male" weapons. They are wielded aggressively, and they pertain to the masculine realm of fighting, war, and the hunt. They were and are essential for carving meat. From a symbolic point of view the knife is phallic.

Knife blades were reduced to one cutting edge sometime in the 17th century. Points were rounded to prevent them from being used as toothpicks and probably to discourage quarrels and assassinations at meals. In 17th century France it became illegal for cutlers to make pointed knives. These changes speeded up the wider use of the fork. Because the knife could no longer be used to spear and convey food to the mouth, the emphasis was now on keeping the fingers and table clean, so the fork helped bring manners to the dining table.

In classical Greece and Rome servants brought the meat already cut, dispensing with the need for knives at the table. Forks were used in the kitchen only for transferring meat from one dish to another for the skewering. Conveying food to the mouth was done by fingers only.*

The brothers Adam, whose innovative and imaginative designs of architecture, furniture, candelabra, etc. had such an impact on English life in the latter half of the 18th century, also markedly changed the social customs during this period. They raised the levels of decoration greatly which in turn raised entertaining and social events to new heights and with them – manners. Concurrently, with the influences of the Adam brothers was that of the English potters such as Josiah Wedgwood, who produced attractive pottery dinnerware that was within the means of a rising middle class. Elizabethan pewter was being replaced by Georgian silver and fine dinnerware. Complete sets of cutlery for dining and entertaining became a necessity and guests no longer were required to furnish their own. Traveling sets

Necessaire; French, c. 1760. Eating tools carried by a traveler. The knife and fork unscrew. Bashford collection.

were still the custom for use at inns and hostelries where all cutlery was not supplied.

While most useful English customs eventually found their way to the "Colonies", the general use of the knife, fork, and spoon occurred somewhat later in America; especially on the rough and ready frontiers. Even carving knives were not common. As Isabella Bird, noted social historian of this period, observed when she dined at a Chicago hotel in 1856, "*There were no carv-*

ing knives, so each person 'hacked' the joint with his own knife. And some of those present carved them dexterously with Bowie knives taken out of their belt."**

As Europe became more civilized the knife or dagger lost much of its importance for hunting or defense, but retained its usefulness for eating. In many countries it became an article of dress, i.e., the Scottish dirk.

During the evolution of the knife and its uses it went from a straight to a curved blade, from two to one cutting edge, and from a pointed to a rounded tip. The centuries of evolution of the knife as a cutting tool to one with two tines on the end made it easier to slice and spear the meat. This tined knife really had no relationship to the introduction of the Italian fork into England in the early 17th century, but did help keep the fingers and table cleaner.

With time, the narrow spindly knife handles were gradually replaced by broader handles whose fanned out ends became a perfect place for crests, initials, and various decorations. By the 18th century knife handles had become works of art, being made of agate, polychrome, ceramic, gold, silver, glass, ebony, and many other fine materials. They were often designed to impress guests with the wealth or status of the host.

Electroplating was introduced in 1840 which made it possible to place silver on base metals such as brass or nickel. Then in 1914 stainless steel was introduced into the manufacture of

trate this.

*** The Bowie knife: origin is attributed to Rezin P. Bowie, brother of James. The knife became very popular on the frontier after James had successfully defended himself with it in a fight at Natchez, Mississippi, September 19, 1825. As demand for the knife grew British manufacturers produced it in large quantities for the American market. James was later to be immortalized by his death at the American stand at the Alamo in 1836.*

cutlery, nearly eliminating the polishing of "silverware" and reducing the need and use of servants, but accelerating the demise of the use of knife rests.

*In ancient Roman homes food was to be eaten only with the right hand. People trained themselves to lean on their left hand or elbow to discourage reaching for food with the left. See paintings, scenes, etc.., of Roman life which illustrate this.

I eat my peas with honey
I've done it all my life.
It makes the peas taste funny
But it keeps 'em on the knife.

The Fork

Dr. Lynn White, professor emeritus of history at the University of California, Los Angeles, and a authority on medieval technology, has said all the world is divided into three parts: "finger feeders", "chop stick feeders", and "fork feeders". Demographically the fork feeders of the world are outnumbered two to one. However, in this chapter we shall dwell only on *"We of the fork"*.

The first fork is mentioned as having been used in the 11th century in Italy. Then use gradually spread to Spain and France, but it took over 500 hundred years before an Englishman announced, on returning home, he'd seen forks in Italy. This Englishman, Thomas Coryat, after a long sojourn in Italy, is generally credited with introducing the fork into England around 1601. The earliest known reference to the use of forks at an English table was made in 1611. London's Victoria and Albert Museum has a fork with two prongs hallmarked 1632 which is possibly the earliest hallmarked fork to be made in Britain.

Forks had been used in Italy for centuries, especially in Venice because, *"The Italian cannot by any means endure to have his dish touched by fingers; seeing all men's fingers are not alike clean."* They were in widespread use by the 16th century and it was from here (most likely via France to England) that the practice of eating with the knife and fork in the modern manner was introduced to the rest of Europe.

As the medieval times came to an end, the use of forks spread rapidly throughout Europe. It was at the famous Tour d'Argent restaurant in Paris* that Henry III spotted two elegant Florentines eating with those "curious instruments", whereupon he immediately abandoned the customary hand-to-mouth habit. After the 11th century date of the first extant document describing (with wonder) the sight of someone using only the fork it took 8 centuries to become a utensil employed universally in the West.

The spread of the use of the fork to the West, its eventual adoption by all the diners, and their use not only to hold food still while it was being cut, but to carry it to one's mouth, brought about its general use.

There are no traces of forks being used during Saxon or medieval times in England though it is worth noting that an Anglo-Saxon silver fork and spoon dating from the 9th century were found in England. And it is possibly the earliest eating fork to have been discovered in Europe.

There is literary evidence that the fork was used by the Greeks and Romans mostly for transferring food from one dish to another. A two tined fork of gold was brought to Italy by a Greek princess in 1071 and forks were listed in personal inventories from the 11th century on. In the 14th century it was common to have one table fork with sets of knives. The fork was to be used for serving only; knives and fingers were used for eating.

As knives became specialized eating tools only, and some began to be made with tines on the end to spear and convey the slice of meat to the mouth, the fork evolved as a separate tool. Two tined forks seemed to have appeared first, but forks with three, four, and even five tines evolved very early.

While table or serving forks came into more or less general use on the tables of the rich and wellborn, not even kings provided eating implements for their guests. Many a crowned head, including Queen Elizabeth I (1533-1603) and Louis XIV of France (1658-1715), ate with their fingers.

Historian, Rhea Tannahill, in her fine book *Food in History*, Stein & Day, 1971, writes, *"Forks were used for many years in Europe and the Near East but only as kitchen implements."* She also ascribes the use of small forks as eating instruments to the Byzantines in the 10th century.

Forks and chopsticks found favor because they made it easier to handle hot food. Before their advent people generally scooped food from hot dishes on pieces of bread.

Forks had only to be seen in use, and their advantages were successfully argued. They

Knife & fork on left-Sheffield 1776, center fork-London 1778, knife & fork on right-Sheffield 1781

then had to be made and sold, produced in forms and quantities which more and more people could afford, as they ceased to being merely necessary and became the mark of civilized behavior.

A major change in eating habits and table manners took place during the second half of the 17th century when table forks became fashionable in England. Their use allowed, even demanded, cleaner and neater eating habits. A diner no longer had to spear meat with a knifepoint, or tear it apart with the fingers, or "sup" messes from a spoon. Consequently there was no longer any need for the monotonous daily diet of stews and similarly sloppy dishes.

Alice Morse Earle, in her book *Home Life in Colonial Times*, gives Governor John Winthrop of Boston, credit for bringing the first fork to the Colonies in 1633 along with a knife and a bodkin in a leather case. Two tined forks of iron and silver were later brought from England and used in New York and Virginia, as well as Massachusetts. The first mention of a single fork in Virginia appears in an inventory dated 1677.

By the late Georgian Period (1760-1820) tableware had begun to assume much the same appearance as we know it now. By Victorian times a whole army of implements were required for a proper meal. Their variety led to such specialized pieces as asparagus tongs and the lobster pick – a far cry from the days not long gone when a man's knife, fork, spoon, or his fingers, did duty for a whole meal.

The unease of a diner, that such an elaborately set table must have often created, might well have been summed up by Oscar Wilde's purported lament, *"The world was my oyster, but I used the wrong fork."*

Rhea Tannahill writes that as late as 1897, *"Sailors in the British Navy were forbidden the use of knives and forks because they were regarded as being prejudicial to discipline and manliness."*

As little as 3 centuries ago most Europeans still used their fingers, regarding forks as foppish, decadent, or worse. French historian Fernand Brandel tells of one medieval German preacher who condemned the fork as *"A diabolical luxury; God would not have given us fingers if he wished us to use such an instrument."*

The use of individual forks began to spread in the 17th century. During this time hard plates, taking the place of soft pewter and wooden trenchers, prerequisites for the constant use of knives and forks, began to be provided for every diner in the homes of the nobles, gentry, and those who could afford them. Let us remember that it would be some time before the lower levels of society in England provided knives, forks, and spoons for their guests. In the meantime, as a guest, you were still expected to provide your own knife to slice meat from the roast or loin and convey it to your mouth with the knife or your fingers. There was much opposition to forks even in high places. One opponent said, *"People would rather touch their mouths with their fingers than with these little forked instruments."*

Arguments against the fork included danger to the lips; it was an awkward and unsightly gesture; it was difficult to get food on the fork; it made for slower eating and forced one to take smaller mouthfuls. The latter two objections really became positive as manners became more *de rigeur*. Men were generally less ready to accept the use of the fork because it was considered foreign and effeminate.

Americans were continually reminded *"Always feed yourself with a fork; a knife is only used as a divider. Use a dessert spoon in eating tarts, puddings, curries, etc.."*

"Put down the knife and take the fork in the right hand.", was the constant reminder in American books of etiquette; often with illustrations.

When and how much the manufacturer influenced manners or vice versa, is difficult to separate. The two combined to create silver chests as big as a colonial highboy, and at the peak of the load on an ambitious and/or willing housewife sets of silver numbered 300 pieces, yes, even 500. More than 150 different types to account for

– i.e., fish, soup, dessert, etc., were produced.

From the <u>London Daily Telegraph</u> of October 29, 1982: "Frances' Tour d'Argent restaurant; opened in 1582 as a modest Paris inn where forks were first introduced to the finger licking North Europeans; celebrated its 400th anniversary yesterday."

The Spoon

Spoon – the word is derived from the Anglo-Saxon word meaning "splinter". In German it is "span" meaning a shaving of wood.

Spoons were made in a great variety of styles and for a great variety of purposes. To name a few: "caddy" spoons with a short handle were used for measuring tea from a caddy (canister), "snuff" spoons were carried in snuffboxes or etuis, "incense" spoons for placing incense in the burner. There was a spoon for nearly every need, occasion or event such as the English Coronation spoon for anointing the new sovereign.

Cutlery handles were made of ivory, silver, gold, wood, agate, jade, rock crystal, silver gilt, porcelain, jasper, and faience. Sheffield was the cutlery center in England beginning in the 17th century and pieces made there are usually hallmarked. On the Continent, the finest

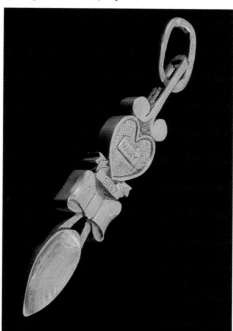

Wooden Welsh loving spoon. Rockwell collection.

cutlery was made at Augsburg, Germany but alas, is rarely marked.

The earliest spoon was a cupped human hand. Every race on earth has made itself spoons of sea shells, coconut shells, bones, gourds, amber, ivory, stones – ranging from agate to jasper, and many types of wood, metal, porcelain, tortoise shell, and horn. Spoons have been used by all people everywhere. Their form is often exceptionally beautiful. They are often considered romantic symbols; people give spoons rather than knives or forks for an anniversary or special occasion. Spoons are often decorated to the expense of usefulness, limiting their utilitarian use, but increasing their beauty and value. Spoons lost their practical use as they became more ceremonial and sentimental.

Well into the 18th century spoons took many shapes – for ladling, stirring, etc.. Some were made just for stirring. Good etiquette forbids leaving your teaspoon in your cup – they are for stirring only. Spoons for everyone meant no more lifting soup bowls to drink their contents and remained the common means of scooping stews and mushy foods from a common pot. Like the cutlery handle, early spoons were made from many different materials. Primitive people still use cup shaped leaves and in many Latin American countries flat food, such as tortillas, are used to scoop up soft foods. The first spoons in Occidental history were fig shaped with a short handle, but its round cup shape has always existed. The Greeks and Romans made them of silver and bronze and during the

From a painting by Petier Breugel (Belgian artist 1564-1638). Note: He proudly displays and carries his treasured spoon in the brim of his cap.

Middle Ages, horn, wood, brass, and pewter were shaped into spoons. The present form of the spoon's bowl had pretty much evolved by 1750.

Until the late 18th century in Europe, when cutlery was provided for all diners, guests often brought their own spoon, as well as their own knife. They served themselves from the liquid dishes with their spoons. Spoons had become common in France by the late 17th century, having been introduced from Italy.

"Apostle" spoons, which often come in sets of 12, were popular as presents at christenings, especially if the person christened was named for an Apostle. They were given as gifts for other festive occasions especially in Germany and the Netherlands. Other designs were popular gifts for weddings and anniversaries.

Long after the advent of the knife and several centuries after the introduction of the fork, the spoon became an established eating tool. Though certainly used in some form by man since the beginning of time in feeding himself, it only evolved into its present form of a small bowl with an attached handle about 1750 and earned third spot in the cutlery trio during the last half of the 18th century in England. The knife was long in place, the fork evolved from the knife and by the beginning of the 19th century, all three tools had pretty much taken the forms as we know them today.

While the spoon was the last to become permanent in the trio of utensils that evolved to make up our present day cutlery, they must have been an important utensil even in the poorest of households. How else to convey hot soup to one's mouth? Surely the vast majority of spoons were of wood, later iron and brass, most of which would not survive. What has survived is silver, used by people of rank and/or affluence. When worn beyond use, they were not thrown away, but melted down.

The colonists had spoons, and certainly all needed them, for at that time much of their food was in the form of soup or "soup meat" such as could be eaten with spoons when there were no forks. Meat was made into hashes or ragouts; thick stews and soups with chopped vegetables and meats were common. The cereal foods, which formed a large part of English fare in the New World, were more frequently boiled in porridge then baked in loaves. Many Indian tribes excelled at making spoons from horns. Better homes had a few silver spoons. Worn-out pewter spoons and dishes could be recast into new spoons or dishes.

And finally, let us remember this admonition from The Life of Johnson; *"When he leaves our house, let us count our spoons."*

The Brilliant Period

The "Brilliant Period" of glass manufacture in the United States represents the finest achievements of the American glassmaker. It is important to the collector of glass knife rests, for most certainly your collection includes some made – unknown to you – during this period. Probably they carry no sign of identification other than the brilliance of the glass.

The Brilliant Period not only produced the finest glass and crystal, but it was a time when entertaining and dining in high style were in their zenith. The American glassmakers rose to the occasion to produce the sparkling crystal that complemented the silver cutlery, English china, and candelabra all laid upon starched white linen tablecloths of the elegant dining tables of that period.

Among the many glass companies of this period, a few stand out: *The Libbey Glass Co., T. G. Hawkes & Co.,* and *J. Hoare & Co.* produced some of the best crystal of the period, whose creations are much sought after today.

Libbey, who began as the *New England Glass Co.* in Massachusetts, in 1818, was beset in 1887 by a strike of their workers. The company chose to move to Toledo, Ohio, a good rail center where there was also a rich deposit of sandstone nearby

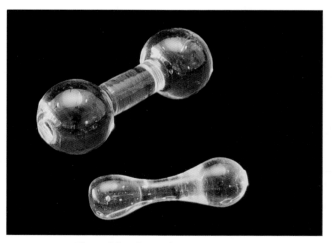

Glass blanks prior to cutting.

high in silica content. Even more important, it was near a recently tapped source of natural gas to provide energy so important to the melting and manufacture of glass. A new factory was built, production began May 16, 1888, and in 1892 the company took the new name of the *Libbey Glass Company*; operating today as the *Owens Illinois Glass Company.*

Its production, weighty with a high lead content that gives it the brilliance of prisms, sharp clarity of cutting and plasticity, are now much sought after by collectors. Edward Drummond Libbey provided money for the construction, maintenance, and free entry to the current magnificent Libbey Museum of Glass in Toledo which should be on everyone's "must visit" list.

The *Libbey* catalogs of 1896, 1904, 1908, and 1909 show some superb examples of their knife rests cut in such patterns as "Princess", "Harvard", "Corinthian", and "Lapidary". Nearly all were etched *Libbey** but even the unmarked productions of this factory can be recognized by the weight of their high lead content, nearly twice that of others.

The second of the acclaimed trio, Thomas G. Hawkes,** born in Ireland, who came to the U. S. at age 17, and learned glass cutting while working for the *Hoare and Dailey Company* in

Brooklyn, Rochester, and Corning, New York. He had become Hoare's superintendent but left in 1880 to start his own firm in Corning. Hawkes died in 1913 but not before he'd been acclaimed one of the great glass cutters of the Brilliant Period.

The *Hawkes* firm continued in business until 1982. Its 1902 catalog shows three knife rests but their production ceased at the end of World War I. The company was basically a cutting firm for blanks made by glass manufacturers such as *Corning* and *Steuben*.

When John Hoare*** came to the U. S. in 1853 from Cork, Ireland, he was already a highly trained glass cutter, having learned the trade in England and from his father in Ireland. He found immediate employment and by 1856 had saved enough money to start his own cutting firm in New York City. In 1868 he moved his factory to Corning, New York, where it survived until 1920.

Again, the *John Hoare Company* was a cutting firm, buying or taking blanks from glass manufacturers and then offering their handiwork (cutting) to the market. Their 1896 catalog shows three knife rests in "Lapidary", "Russian", and "Signora" patterns. In their 1911 catalog are six knife rests, having added the "Monarch", "Regular", and "Prism" patterns. The company had an exhibit at the Columbian Exposition in Chicago in 1893 where it offered its claim, "The Pioneers of Cut Glass".

This trio made some of the finest examples of cut crystal knife rests seen anywhere. The quality of the crystal, eye-catching designs, and sharpness of cuts are superb. Certainly other manufac-turers produced excellent glass knife rests during this period, but many can't be ascribed to any particular maker.

Since glass knife rests did not become a prominent part of the American dining scene until the Brilliant Period of cut glass, when dating of their manufacture and use was certain, any dates given other glass knife rests are hypothetical.

While the sales catalogs and other printed information of the companies of this period are mostly gone, some are preserved; enough to give a good overview of the industry. There were few glass manufacturers, but many cutters who also sold their handiwork. Not all offered knife rests in their catalogs.

Here is a list of the well known glass factories of the Brilliant Period beginning in 1856 through 1903. If not cutting their own knife rests, they were almost certainly making and supplying blanks of various items to the many cutting shops. In 1903, *C. Dorflinger & Sons* were supplying glass blanks to 22 cutters in Wayne County, Pennsylvania alone, almost certainly some of these blanks must have become knife rests.

Name of the Company	Year Founded
J. Hoare & Co., Corning, New York	1856*
C. Dorflinger & Sons, White Mills, Pennsylvania	1860**
Mt. Washington Glass Co., New Bedford, Massachusetts	1869
Pitkin & Brooks, Chicago, Illinois	1872
Meriden Cut Glass Co., Meriden, Connecticut	1876**
T. G. Hawkes & Co., Corning, New York	1880*

Pairpoint Corp.,
    New Bedford, Massachusetts   1880*
T. B. Clark & Co.,
    Honesdale, Pennsylvania   1884*
Libbey Glass Co., Toledo, Ohio   1888*
J. D. Bergen Co., Meriden, Connecticut   1893*
Empire Glass Co.,
    Flemington, New Jersey   1895**
O. F. Egglinton Co., Corning, New York   1896*
Sterling Glass Co., Cincinnati, Ohio   1900
Tuthill Glass Co., Middletown, New York   1900
H. C. Fry Glass Co.,
    Rochester, Pennsylvania   1901
H. P. Sinclaire & Co.,
    Corning, New York****   1903*
Steuben, Corning, New York   1903
Quaker City Cut Glass Co.

*companies whose reprinted catalogs are available and show knife rests
**reprint shows no knife rests

The 1913 catalog of the prominent Cincinnati wholesaler of *Wallenstein, Mayer & Co.* shows, among other cut glass table items, a standard lapidary knife rest – price $ .70 each. Knife rests, like glass salts, and napkin rings, being of minor importance to the dining scene, were apparently incidental and did not necessarily have to match the other cut crystal used in the setting. Therefore, they could be purchased separately. Sets were made of salts, napkin rings, and knife rests with matching cut designs.

As the wide variety of fascinating patterns show, these useful items may have been examples

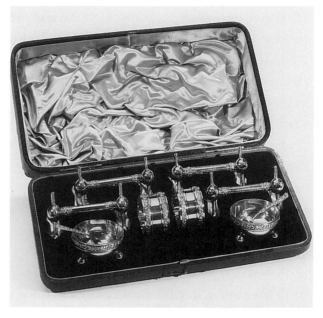

An attractive boxed set of knife rests, salts and napkin rings for the host and hostess. The items are not silver but probably fine nickel plate. Rockwell collection.

of the fanciful imaginations of the designers and cutters. Blanks from which the pressed knife rests were to be made were cast in molds of different sizes. The glass was poured, allowed to cool and harden, the riser broken off, and the blanks then sold, sent to outside cutters, or retained for in-house engraving.

The excellent glass of this period was called "brilliant" for a good reason. Not only had glassmaking techniques in America equaled those of England and the Continent, but were now superior. Composed of the standard ingredients, sand (silica), potash, lime, glassmakers soap and cullet, oxide of lead was added in varying amounts which provided the brilliance of the facets, the prism of colors from sunlight through the cut surface, and easier sharper cutting. Standard crystal contained 24-26% lead, while *Libbey*, which has a brilliance all its own, contained 42-44% lead. *Libbey* knife rests can often be identified by holding two of similar size. *Libbey* is likely to be the heavier of the two. Try this for yourself.

It is well to know that most of the glass companies of the so-called Brilliant Period were cutting houses. There were only a few manufacturers. In 1909 Thomas Hawkes founded the *Steuben Glass Company* in Corning, New York, to assure himself of an adequate and continuous supply of blanks.

Other manufacturing firms of this period include the *New England Glass Company* (later to become *Libbey* in Toledo), the *Boston and Sandwich Glass Company* and the *Mt. Washington Glass Company*, all in Massachusetts.

Such was the amazing popularity and demand for this glass which, until its perfection, had to compete with the cheaper and prestigious imported glass. Often called "flint glass" or "rock crystal", colors were produced by the use of metallic oxides.

Many of the glass companies used paper labels now long gone, making exact identification difficult. Some existing companies may have records of their parent companies; the two great glass museums, *Corning* in Corning, New York and *Libbey* in Toledo, have information in depth and are glad to share it. The American Cut Glass Association. P. O. Box 482, Ramona, CA 92065, has reprints of catalogs of the late 19th and early 20th century glass companies of which nine show their knife rests. The catalogs are for sale, but check your local library before ordering any.

About 1910, and accelerated by WWI, the popularity of cut glass began a slow decline accompanied, coincidentally, by the decline in the use of the knife rest. The Brilliant Period, its beginning signaled by the end of the Civil War and the consequent rebuilding of the American economy, the rise of a wealthy middle class and the metamorphosis of a social order that demanded and could afford a better life style drew

to a close, leaving the superb glass which collectors seek today. May you be fortunate to have some knife rests of this period.

*Carl U. Fauster, the recognized authority on Libbey writes in a letter dated October 5, 1965, "Concerning the significance of the sword as part of the Libbey trademark, the writer has never been able to determine whether this was adopted because Libbey was made in Toledo, named after the Spanish city famous for swords, or whether the sword was meant to be a cutlass signifying cut glass."

**Thomas G. Hawkes, who had established a cutting firm in Corning, New York, had, since 1880, been importing glass blanks from the Stevens & Williams factory in England. He persuaded Frederick Carder, then a rising glassmaker at Stevens & Williams, to come to the United States in 1903 where Hawkes set Carder up in Corning,

New York as the Stuben Glass Company. Hawkes wanted a source of blanks in the U.S. and guaranteed he'd take all the blanks Carder could produce.

*** Called "Captain Hoare" by his associates and employees.

****Henry P. Sinclaire joined the Corning Glass Company as a bookkeeper at age 19. He founded his own cutting and engraving firm in 1904. His knife rests are equal to the best of the early 20th century.

Knife Rests on the Continent

Glass – The authors's assembled collection of knife rests made in Europe indicates metal was more popular that glass, but this may not be a true sampling, for glass was made in nearly every industrial European country. Knife rests were part of the dining scene in most of them.

France seems to be the most prolific producer of glass knife rests with such well known companies as *Daum, Sabino, Sèvres, Baccarat,** and *Lalique*** leading the way; aided by such lesser firms as *Etling* and *Verlys*. All are usually signed. The *Sèvres, Baccarat,* and *St. Louis* marks will be acid etched while *Lalique* and *Sabino* marks take the form of engraved signatures. *Lalique* is further identified by their use of frosted

glass: often with the bust of a cupid on either end of the crossbar. The collector should be aware of those pieces that are frosted but not signed. Knife rests of fine *Baccarat* glass are still being made and are available in better shops the world over. *Val St. Lambert**** of Belgium was another major European producer of glass knife rests. Swedish glass has always been held in high es-

teem and her early knife rests are much sought after collector's items.

In a correspondence in 1973 with Robert Charleston, then the curator of the Victoria and Albert Museum arts department and a recognized glass historian, Mr. Charleston noted that knife rests first appeared in Swedish glass pattern books about the middle of the 19th century. In addition

Sèvres: **While more famous for their beautiful china, *Sèvres* manufactured glass beginning in 1727. Through the years the factory produced engraved and art glass and tableware including knife rests. The *Sèvres* glassworks was closed in 1952. This etched mark was first used in 1945.**

he stated that his studies of glass show knife rests illustrated in a Bohemian catalog, c. 1840. He further states that illustrations of German glass show pressed glass knife rests dated 1820.

The glass of Bohemia and Venice has been renowned for centuries. While the author has seen no knife rests positively attributable to those great glass centers there is every reason to believe they were made to complement their fine productions, especially as the presence of eating utensils became "de rigeur" in better homes, and as fine dining became the norm in high society.

*Baccarat, founded in 1765 in a small town 250 miles east of Paris is famed for its glass. The company added a line of crystal glass (24%

lead) in 1817 to its standard lines of regular glass-ware, mirrors, window glass and bottles. It has made and still does make charming knife rests; usually of flat rectangular shapes.

**After 1945 pieces were etched "Lalique, France".

***Founded in 1826, Val St. Lambert became, in the 19th century, one of the three great glass companies of Western Europe. At its zenith between 1879-1914, it had as many as 5000 employees and produced up to 160,000 items daily; with sales worldwide. About 1900 the company ceased production of knife rests, only to resume manufacture in February, 1992.

Ceramic – With ceramic knife rests in Europe, France seems again to lead the way possibly because her many potteries, in production for centuries, have been very well chronicled. Many books have been written, articles and experts on French ceramics abound, and some factories are still in production. To this day knife

rests are being manufactured and sold for use at meals in better homes.

Firms in Quimper, Limoges,* Rouen, and Moustiers have been the most productive and

with the majority of rests being tin-glazed,** Rouen, Quimper and Moustiers (near Marseilles) were the faience manufacturing centers of French

knife rests. Other factories producing ceramic knife rests in the 18th, 19th, and 20th centuries include *Sèvres, Etling, Longwy, Nevers, Sarreguemines, Malicorne, Angouleme, Strasbourg, Boulogne – sur-Mer, Desvres,* and *Robj.****

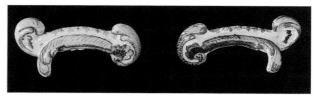

Villeroy and *Boch* (1856) and *Meissen* of Dresden in Germany are still producing knife rests today, while *Herend,* Hungary's long time stellar potter, made rests.

It is well to keep in mind that the location or country where you buy your gems (knife rests) does not mean they are made there. Trade between the European countries went on for centuries and was particularly brisk during the reign of Queen Victoria. This was a period of unprecedented peace and prosperity for Europe. It was also the time of the rise of dining as a major social event, and a period of the great popularity of knife rests, usually in pairs. They could be English or Continental. Be skeptical of dealer's claims to dates and places of manufacture. True identification comes from impressed or stamped marks or from factory catalogs. To add your personal touch, do some research on your own.

*Evidence indicates several potteries in Limoges were producing knife rests as early as the 17th century 'til early in the 20th century. Havi-

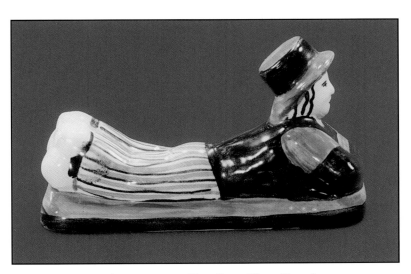

Quimper — Rockwell collection

land, one of the potteries in Limoges produced knife rests between 1865-1930 when the factory was closed.

**Mailoica in Italy, delftware in England, and faience in France has an opaque white glaze from its powdered tin. Since the glaze did not flow in firing, decorations could be painted on without fear of them running. In fact, the colors would meld into the glaze. Not all colors could stand the high heat, hence a limit to those used in decorating.

***This name, Robj, backstamped on each knife rest, is the anagram of Jean Born, founder of this French company in 1910 in Paris. He did no manufacturing but instead bought from, or commissioned, manufacturers of acclaimed artistic items, especially during the Art Deco period. Several French potteries were part of his operation. Included were Limoges factories and these rests were probably produced there in the 1920s.

Metal While ceramic appears to have been a very popular medium for knife rests in France, followed closely by glass, metal seemed to have been the choice of Europe as a whole.

The cause of cutlery was advanced by the discovery and use of steel in Italy in the late 15th and early 16th centuries. Its use and manufacture spread to Germany, particularly in Augsburg and Nurnberg. Steel cutters, very skilled and

ture, craft guilds evolved which when fully recognized, created regulations governing the silver and gold content of cutlery, as well as the admission of craftsmen to a guild. These marks enable present day collectors to identify maker, location, etc..

"Man seldom thinks with more earnestness of anything than he does of his dinner"

"Bad men live to eat and drink, whereas good men eat and drink in order to live."
Socrates, 469-399 B. C.

very few, became the darlings of cutlery manufacture.

The premier French manufacturer of metal knife rests and cutlery has been *Christofle* of St. Denis, near Paris, founded in 1830. Made of an alloy of nickel and zinc, this company claims each piece carries 50% more gleaming silver plate than the best American flatware. Their knife rests and attractive plated animal shapes are usually signed.

After several centuries of silver manufac-

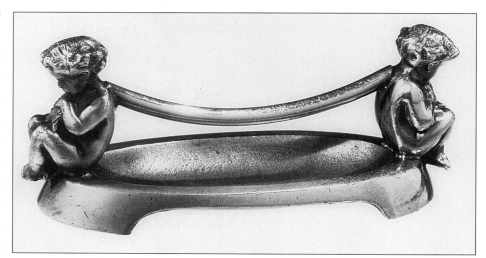

Map of French Potters

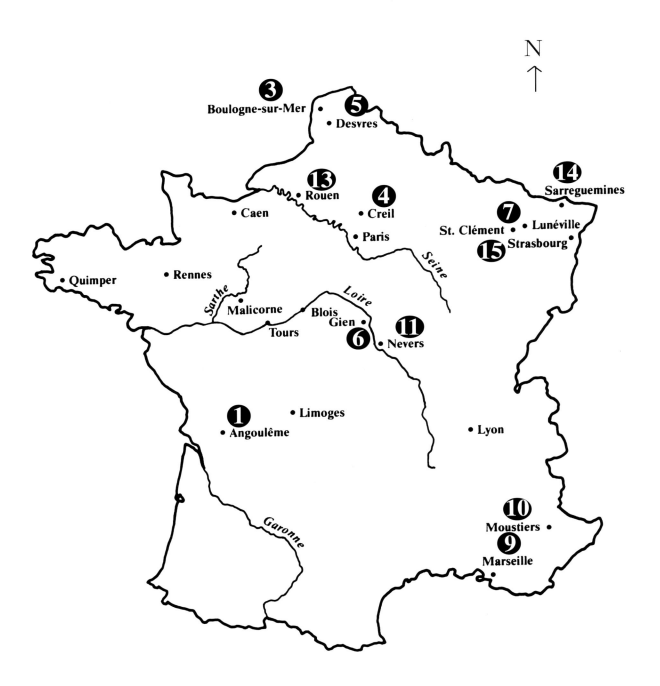

N
↑

3
Boulogne-sur-Mer •
5
• Desvres

13
• Rouen
4
• Caen
• Creil
• Paris

14
Sarreguemines
•

7
St. Clément •
• Lunéville
15
• Strasbourg

• Quimper
• Rennes

Seine

Loire
Sarthe
• Malicorne
Blois
Gien •
Tours
6
• Nevers
11

1
• Limoges
• Angoulême

• Lyon

Garonne

10
Moustiers •

9
Marseille

French Potters

❶ Angoulème

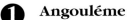 Lassuze 1882   Pineau and Patros 1888   Renoleau (1900-1930)

❷ Blois

Ulysse à Blois

(1861-1889)

 Ulysse Blois E Balon Se^{rs}

(1890-1929)

Ulysse à Blois
G Bruneau Balon
S^{re} d'E. Balon

G. Bruneau-Balon=Blois

(1930)

J. Tortat BLOIS

(1873-1881)

Adrien Thibault (1875-1918)

❸ Boulogne

 Verlingue (1903-1920)   Louis & Verlingue (1910)   Henri Delcourt (1920 -   )

❹ Creil Montereau

 1880   TL CREIL    creil et Montereau.

❺ Desvres

  Formaintraux-Courquin (1872-1934)   Fourmaintraux frères (1877-1887)

 Gabriel Fourmaintraux (1900-1934)

 FAIENCERIE D'ART
Décor Main

MASSE FRÈRES
DESVRES

 Géo Martel (1900-   )

❻ Gien

(1856-1860) (1860-1871)

ɔnt.

1871-1875 1875-1935

1938-1960 1941-1960 1960-1971 since 1971

❼ Luneville St. Clement

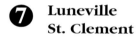   

Currently in use with date

❽ Malicorne

Pouplard/Béatrix
(1895-1952)

Tessier
(1924-in current use)

❾ Marseilles

Veuve Perrin
(1748-1795)

Twentieth century reproductions continue to use this mark.

❿ Moustiers
in current production

De Peyre
Feret
J.M.V. Fine
Garnier

Morée-Méret
St. Michel
de Ségriès
Stefani á St. Jurs

Martes-Tolosane

Reproductions of
Moustiers designs

⓫ Nevers

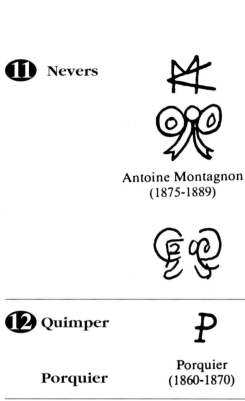

Antoine Montagnon
(1875-1889)

Antoine Montagnon
(1889-1899)

F.E. Cottard
1922

Gabriel Montagnon
(1899-1937)

Jean Montagnon
(1937-1978)

⓬ Quimper

Porquier

P

Porquier
(1860-1870)

Porquier (Beau)
(1875-1905)

Adolph Porquier
(1875-1905)

**de la
Hubaudière
Grande Maison
HB**

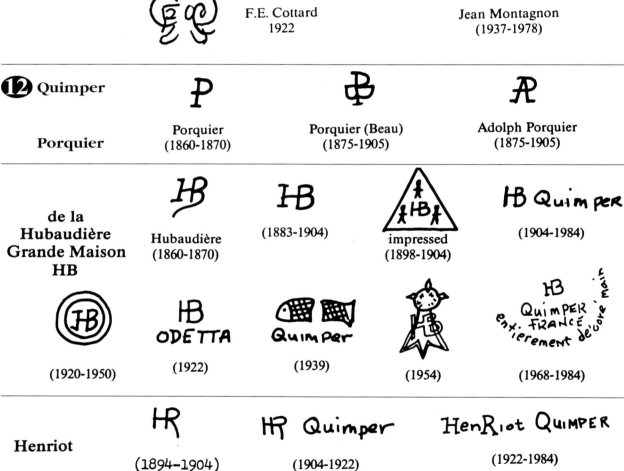

Hubaudière
(1860-1870)

(1883-1904)

impressed
(1898-1904)

HB Quimper
(1904-1984)

(1920-1950)

HB ODETTA
(1922)

Quimper
(1939)

(1954)

(1968-1984)

Henriot

HR
(1894-1904)

HR Quimper
(1904-1922)

HenRiot Quimper
(1922-1984)

 Quimper
(1915-1930s)

(1968-1984)

(1984-   )

Marks used on items commissioned for a particular shop

FRANCE QUIMPER

Made by HB for
Macy's New York
in the 1930s

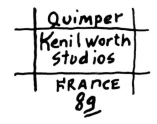

Made for Kenilworth
Studios (?) by
HenRiot in the 1930s

N. S. & . S
HB
QUIMPER
FRANCE
• • •

Made for N.S & .S (?)
by HB in the 1930s

FIRESIDE
HenRiot
Quimper
FRANCE

Usually on yellow items

Fouillen

P. Fouillen
QuiMPER

Keraluc

Keraluc
prés QuimPER

⓭ Rouen

See Tardy for a long list of 18th century marks.

(in blue, often accompanied by a number in black)
Late 19th or 20th century reproduction; probably Desvres.

⓮ Sarreguemines

1800-1850

19th century

SARREGUEMINES
SARREGUEMINES
DIGION
SARREGUEMINES ET
FRANCE

1876

D representing the addition of Dignon
V representing the addition of Vitry
1880

⓯ Stasbourg

See Tardy for 18th century marks.
Reproductions made currently by Lunéville St. Clément.

Manners

It is one of the premises underlying this book that no society exists without table manners, and especially, without rules that govern

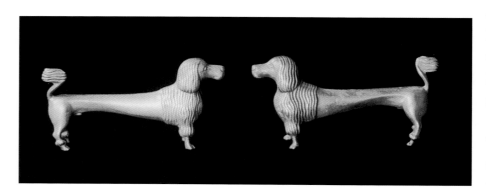

eating behavior. Table manners are politeness where food is concerned, and are social agreements that help make our lives easier because they set other people at ease. We are accepted when we display good manners.

Another of the reasons for "manners" is precisely that they pressure people to behave in a predictable pattern. We all know what to do on given occasions, a funeral, a wedding, a family affair, thus making these occasions more meaningful. Rituals are there to make difficult occasions easier. Since eating almost always occurs at these events, manners are essential.

Polite behavior is ritual performed for the sake of other people – and our own well being. A polite person is a polished person.

> *"Men are polished through act and speech,*
> *each by each*
> *As pebbles are smoothed on a rolling*
> *beach."*

Manners are a form of communication and by using them we show our companions we understand. We are accepted because we know and act according to a set of rules and behavior. *"Every meal,"* goes a Victorian proverb, *"is a lesson learned."* Table manners are rituals because they are the way in which it is com-

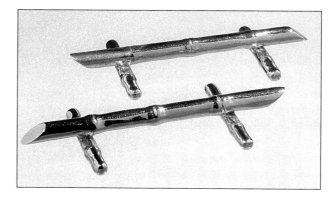

monly agreed that eating should be performed.

Manners have indeed changed but slowly and often in the face of long and widespread unwillingness, i.e., using forks instead of fingers – which took decades, in fact centuries, for people to generally follow suit. During the 17th century in France manners became a political issue. King Louis XIV and successors instituted a sort of school of manners, and the courtiers had better attend and practice manners, or else.

Manners and order at dinner reflected on the host/hostess. The subsequent remarks or gossip by guests labeled the host/hostess. In 1837 an American expert on behavior wrote that it takes three generations to learn how to behave, to acquire the manners and social veneer necessary for acceptance.

In the 19th century, etiquette manuals poured off the presses in the U. S.. They offered advice on how to be "refined" based on English and French models. But beyond the Eastern seaboard, life and society were still pretty raw and not given to social niceties.

In the 20th century a whole new generation of etiquette manuals began to appear. The doyenne (leader, social expert and exponent of civility) was Emily Post, who produced *"Etiquette in Society, in Business, in Politics, and at Home"* in 1922. It became the bible of the hostess for several generations. It also played an im-

portant part in establishing manners through all strata of American society. Today it is Judith Martin, "Miss Manners", whose syndicated column appears in many papers, which supplies her readers a system of etiquette that is demanding and precise.

Table manners have a history, ancient and complex, and each society has gradually evolved its own system. In spite of differences, table manners, all things considered, are remarkably similar both historically and currently the world over.

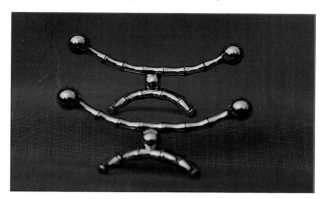

Where people ate with their hands from a common dish, it was etiquette that nothing bitten should be put back. It must be entirely eaten by the person who took it. We should not be led to assume that people who habitually eat with their

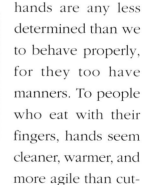

hands are any less determined than we to behave properly, for they too have manners. To people who eat with their fingers, hands seem cleaner, warmer, and more agile than cutlery.

When we are young, older people have the field. They are in charge and in power. All must learn their manners if we want to be invited to dinner by them. Because table manners are drummed into us so early and so insistently, the rules upon which they are based rarely need to be remembered once we have grown up. We have made them part of the way we habitually act. In Anglo-Saxon culture one of the first lessons children learn is to say "thank you". Thanking people is still one of the most important rules of etiquette and good manners. The English nobility educated their children by exchanging them, after about the age of eight, with children of other aristocratic households so they could be disciplined outside their homes.

There are many taboos connected with dining and quite a few concerned the knife. It was after all, the lion among the dining tools. It was never to be pointed at anyone because, as has been stated, "We have only recently learned not to convey food to our mouth with our knife." Knives must be set at the diner's places with the cutting edge of the blades facing in toward the plate. They should never be held upright or in the fist. One's grip on the knife at the table should suggest concentration on the delicate, specific, and entirely necessary operation of eating. When the meal is finished, once again the knife blade

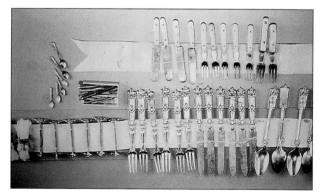

Child's miniature silver set. Note knife rests on the left.

should be set facing the middle of the plate and

not facing our neighbors.

In the 15th century, polite English people were told: *"At meat, cleanse not thy teeth nor pick with knife, or straw, or wand, or stick."*

Three centuries later a slightly more lenient attitude toward toothpicks: *"Pick not thy teeth with thy knife or fingers' end, but a stick or some clean thing – then do ye not offend."*

Manners books that have survived remind people in strong terms, *"It is discourteous to look at others while you are drinking. Mouths must not pout or gape, twist, purse themselves up, or twitch. Do not stare nor look envious (especially with one eye open, the other shut). No leaning left or right and no elbows on the table. Keep both hands on the table or at least in view to avoid being suspected of scratching one's self."* (A real no-no in Continental Europe.)

Two patterns of the formal European dinner evolved and were used in the 15th, 16th, 17th, and 18th centuries. First, dinner à la Francaise: it was divided into two or three courses – "overture", "climax", and the "sweet floral finish"; really soup, meat, and one or two vegetables and dessert. Heaping dishes of food were set on the table along with a thicket of decorations including epergnes, baskets of flowers, ornaments, such as small china figures of men, women, and animals, as well as candelabra. It was crowded and required many serving dishes and a corresponding number of servants.

The second pattern to become popular was the dinner à la Russe: a simpler, less pretentious meal. One dish of food was passed around by servants to be shared by all diners.

Food of course was prepared and brought from the kitchen. The table was less ornately decorated, but this style required an enormous number of serving dishes and a corresponding number of servants.

Both styles found favor in England over the years, the best features of both made up that which was brought to the New World by our Scotch, Welsh, English, Irish, and Cornish forefathers to survive pretty much as we use them today.

Dinners demand control, order and regularity. The home of the host must be in perfect order, for the host was on display along with his meal and its attendant rules of conduct. The guest is sizing up or viewing everything about the home and meal of the host for it will most likely be his turn one day and the roles will be reversed. All this brings order, uniformity and manners to the occasion.

During the 18th and 19th centuries it became common and proper for the diner to retain the appropriate utensil for the dessert. So proper was it to keep one, that a 20th century Canadian waitress is reported to have advised British royalty, *"Keep your fork Duke, there's pie."*

It was not considered good manners to lavishly praise the food or dinnerware or cutlery either in France or England during Georgian and Victorian times. To actually praise the food, states a contemporary French work on manners, *"Makes you look as though you want some more."* Instead, praise could be projected through carefully muted appreciation. A Victorian hostess responding to praise is said to have asked, *"Did you not expect to eat well in my house?"*

Belching, while looked upon as approval of a meal in some cultures, was and is strictly forbidden in Western societies.

Modern dinners pose a dilemma: how to be a good guest and at the same time talk and chew with your mouth closed. Modern Western table manners dictate that eating must be performed with the mouth closed. The rule is extraordinary because we are not expected to observe silence during meals. On the contrary, we consider it impolite, except in very intimate circumstances, not to talk.

There are a few ways which modern hosts can discreetly urge dilatory guests to leave. In Germany a guest must begin making plans to leave when the host ceases to offer a refill; and if the hostess pleads with one to stay, one should do so, but for no longer than 30 minutes. If a French host asks if you would like something, say "fruit juice", the clue that you plan to leave in a short while. A Rumanian host is clearer; he quietly recorks the wine bottle.

An old Arab saying: *"You learn manners by watching those who don't have them."*

> *"When I sat next to the Duchess at tea,*
> *it was just as I knew it would be.*
> *Her rumblings abdominal*
> *were something phenomenal*
> *And everyone thought it was me."*

Social Customs Connected with Dining

The fear of being poisoned haunted the medieval mind. All food offered to certain higher-up people was "assayed" by tasters, who had been trained to perform their task with great deliberation and with an air of utmost unconcern.

Only the most important people had their food tasted for poison; this elaborate ceremony conferring great prestige, being considered important enough for this. Our custom of wine tasting before approval for guests is a reminder of the fear of being poisoned*

Every culture has had certain customs endemic to its eating and its meals. These customs have evolved and have been practiced to bring order to the meal and to emphasize its importance. Again, a reminder that this book is deliberately slanted to reveal the rise of dining and the use of the knife, fork, and spoon in the English speaking world, and with the appearance of the KNIFE REST as a necessary part of the evolution.

In nearly all ages and cultures, talk at the dinner table was almost a necessity. It was rude to eat and not talk, but, at the same time, often difficult to maintain the other rule, *"Do not talk with your mouth full."* Chewing had to be performed with the mouth shut. The Babylonian Talmud (c. AD 450) advises; *"When eating, refrain from speaking lest the windpipe open before*

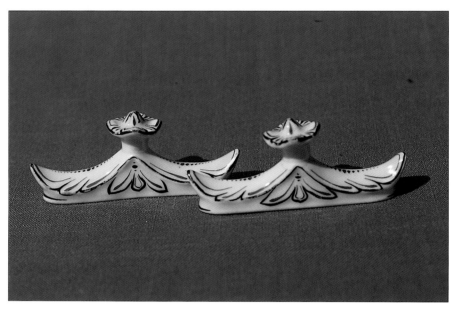

the gullet, and like be in danger." In the 18th century, Lord Chesterfield warned his son that, *"Gentlemen never laugh, they only smile, for laughter makes a disagreeable noise and shockingly distorts the face."* It was good 18th century manners not to draw attention to one's self at the table, not to be loud, not to be embarrassing, not to be repetitious, or boring. One listened even to the most boring talker for, if deemed worthy of an invitation, it was courtesy to listen, at least for the time being.

The carver, where meat was ceremonially cut and divided before the assembled diners, was the focus of everyone's attention. A 16th or 17th century noblemen's education was not complete until he'd learned to carve. He was trained as a youth and performed at the table in full view of the diners and guests to demonstrate his skills. A particularly good performance might bring applause, well earned for the roast might be a whole oxen, stag, goose, hog, pheasant, capon, swan, guinea fowl, or turkey. All of these demanded skill and dexterity. Since the carving and serving were done before persons of high rank or in festive circumstances, the ceremony must look impressive.

It called for the display of the finest cutlery of attractive shapes and designs in gold, silver, ivory, agate, bone, etc., plus specialized knives depending on the kind and size of the roast. Skewers for steadying the meat, later to be large forks, were there. By the 16th century professional carvers were available and by the end of the 18th century servants increasingly did the carving at very formal dinners or occasions. However, the tradition had survived in Britain for the host or father to carve and apportion out the "joint" or roast to the diners. (Thank goodness, for it has maintained a steady supply of knife rests – now our collecting gems.) As late as 1922 Emily Post was complaining that carving was *"an art being lost."*. Even in 1928, she still preferred that carvers should perform while seated, but it was perfectly in order for the cook to carve in the kitchen to keep it warm. By 1945 she (Post) had dropped the section on carving techniques from her handbook on etiquette.

From Elizabethan times women seemed to have carved meat at British tables. They might have done so at the request of the host who might have been slightly incapacitated, or they might have taken carving lessons and seized an opportunity to demonstrate their skills.

Large dinner and formal affairs, very often organized and directed by women, have been an enormous civilizing influence on the history of mankind. Women have been the consciousness raisers in the domain of manners, customs, and consideration for others. They have insisted on proper conduct. They have been bowed to, had hats lifted to them, doors opened, and seats offered. Since 1885 nearly all etiquette books have been written by women.

Toasting was used during the 18th century to force guests to learn each other's names. Everyone knew that when the toasting began, guests would have to lead a toast; calling out their companion's name.

In some cultures, loudly praising the food, smacking one's lips, and so on might be thought to be both polite and thoughtful. Other cultures prefer to stress that food is not everything, and guzzling is disgusting. Sometimes it is correct to be silent; on other occasions one must talk at all costs. Compliments must be sincere, but flattery was vulgar, scandal as gossip a disgrace. Private or indelicate matters must never be mentioned. Ostentatious displays of knowledge, and expounding on one's hobbies and dogmatic opinions must never be voiced. *"Politeness is universal toleration."*

Food was served on platters or "chargers" from which one served himself. Each diner had before him a "trencher", often in the form of a whole slice of bread. He ate his food from it. When finished, the leftovers, together with their meat soaked trenchers were commonly given to the poor, or thrown to the usual raft of dogs and cats in the dining area. Guests, in some circumstances, were encouraged to feed the pets. Many societies still eat their meals off bread, baked broad and flat, like large pancakes.

Servants and other help at a large important dinner could reasonably expect much food not to be eaten. They would eagerly and hungrily await the dinner's end and the return of the uneaten food to the kitchen where it was immediately consumed. After all, refrigeration was unlikely. So the disposal by the help served two ends; excellent food to eat and prevention of spoilage, or need to throw it away.

Table manners everywhere insist on the proper rituals at the beginning of the meal. They impose rules that stifle the impulse to eat the moment your food has been served. Our own (Anglo-Saxon) culture may require a signal from the host or hostess, but generally we are to wait until all have been served.

The dining board, set on a trestle, was replaced by the dining table. Skilled craftsmen made the new table and fashioned it with a central pillar and splayed feet. The table had the capacity to increase or decrease its dimensions depending on the number of diners. The new Georgian silver replaced the Elizabethan pewter.

By the 19th century the dining table became a valuable part of even middle-class household furnishings. Made of rare woods, polished 'til it gleamed, it became, in the late 18th century, another perfect household treasure to show off by removing all coverings and by placing desserts on doilies. Tablecloths were first heard of in Rome at the time of the Emperors. Gradually they became essential to the class and beauty of a banquet table. By the Middle Ages they were more admired than the table itself. Damascus in Syria was where all the best tablecloths were made – hence the word "Damask". Later Irish linens became prized. Table linens were always a mark of class, elegance, and wealth.

With the advent of the Victorian Age (1837-1901) more attention was paid to the formalities of hospitality and formal dining. Dozens of books were published providing strict rules for decorum and deportment, and instructions for details such as setting a table or folding a napkin. Mrs. Beaton's *Household Management*, first published in 1859, was the bible of late Victorian hostesses. It went through 10 editions until the final one in 1952. By 1885 most etiquette books were being written by women.

Increasing wealth and comfort, as well as the influence of French customs, brought about a change in mealtimes. As more people were able to heat and light their homes, they were no longer obliged to retire at sunset and rise at dawn. Consequently, meals were taken later. The Victorian leisured class took breakfast or tea or chocolate with bread and butter at about 10 or 11 a. m.. Dinner was eaten at 5 or 6 p.m., and supper was served late in the evening. The middle classes were deluged with advice from books and magazines. Mrs. Beaton was only the spearhead of a small army of domestic economists.

The Victorian Age, with its poverty for the masses and its prospects of sudden wealth for the successful, was a time of gluttony for many a self-made man. Corpulence became an outward sign of moving up the financial and social ladder.

This was also the age of the rich merchant who needed to display his material success, and the service of meals became more sophisticated. Instead of several meats being served together on a single platter, as one course, each dish was now served separately to each diner in its own covered container by a servant. It was also common for dishes to be placed on the table "family style".

Table utensils and table manners came slowly in Mid-America as the frontier was pushed Westward. The use of the knife, fork, and spoon, china dinner sets, linens, and table accoutrement had long been part of the social and everyday scenes of dining along the Eastern seaboard. It is well to remember that colonial and early American fashions came from the Mother country with the English, Scotch, Welsh, Irish, and Cornish immigrants who came either for a better life or for business and social reasons. The men and women who pushed Westward, after the British finally pulled back into Canada, and the areas west of the Allegheny Mountains were secure from the Indians, and after the opening, in 1825, of the Erie Canal, survival, not social niceties, was paramount.

Eating in the home was simple, with a minimum of utensils. Most meals were centered around the meat dish with local fruits and vegetables available in season. Taverns were available with meals for the traveler. Meals were basic and most amenities we know today were nonexistent.

"A great step toward independence is a good-humored stomach; one that is willing to endure rough treatment."

Seneca, the Roman Philosopher

Individual place settings were based on those described in Miss Catherine Beecher's *Domestic Recipe Book*, a popular volume of recipes and household advice published in 1850. From Miss Beecher and similar sources, it became apparent that both bread-and-butter plates and salad bowls were unknown in the mid 19th century. Knives and forks constituted a set, while spoons were considered more specialized utensils for serving, for eating soup and dessert, and for stirring hot drinks. Carving knives were not common. As Isabella Bird observed when she dined at a Chicago hotel in 1856, *"There were no carving knives, so each person hacked the joints with his own knife, and some of those present carved them dexterously with Bowie knives taken out of their belts."*

Sets of salt and pepper shakers were not yet common. Instead, salt was taken from an open container called a "salt" or salt stand with a tiny spoon or the tip of a knife. Isabella Bird also described this aspect of table d'hote in Chicago, *"Neither were there salt spoons, so everybody dipped his greasy knife in the little pewter pot containing salt."* Pepper was considered a cooking spice, much like cinnamon or ginger. It was used in the kitchen where it might be stored in a cylindrical tin "pepper box" with a handle and pierced top. If a visitor requested, a tin pepper box was brought to his table from the kitchen and after use, was returned to the kitchen.

Industry, commerce, the professions, and

51

a more structured society followed the frontiersmen. Dining became an important social occasion complete with the fine linens, better china, and manners. The Brilliant Period of fine glass (1880-1915) brought its wonderful cut crystal within means of at least middle class Americans. It also brought the fine cut and pressed glass knife rests so highly prized as collector's items today.

*It was only in January of 1989 that the new Emperor of Japan announced that for the first time in Japanese history, there would be no requirement for food tasting before each royal meal.

Decorating

Plating

The discovery of plating one metal on another by an electroplating process occurred about 1840. At later dates plating a metal such as silver on glass and ceramic became accepted practices even in the decorative world. The object to be decorated was given a design often done by a silk screen process which applied a design medium containing powdered silver, a good conductor of electric current. The item to be plated was immersed in an electrolytic bath which both carried and deposited the material from the anode on the object.

Painting*

Most common in France, decorating by skilled painters or paintresses, on the knife rests we now collect, made them especially attractive. They dressed up the dining table while provid-

rests were probably dull oxides when applied. It took the flame and heat of the kiln to force the oxides hidden brilliances to be revealed.

Glass Stippling

A vast number of tiny punched dots delicately done with a very fine diamond or silicon carbide tool.

Glass Engraving

Actually the cutting of a precise pattern to design such as the name of the company or the artist, using a diamond or silicon carbide tool.

Transfer Print Decorating

Many lovely knife rests carrying your favorite blue printed decorations got that way by having a colored design transferred via a printing process to the white body of the rest. Copper plates were made; they were coated with a spe-

ing a palette for the imagination of the decorators. Knife rests of the *Quimper* factories are especially colorful and are still being made there.

You are urged to keep in mind the brilliant colors you see on your beautiful French knife

cial medium containing the color, then wiped clean. A special potter's paper was applied that picked up the design and color. When applied by hand to the intended (almost always earthenware) object with pressure, the design was trans ferred. The paper was removed, the knife rest was dried, dipped in a liquid glaze and fired in a glost kiln. VOILA! You have that lovely bit for your collection.

Acid Etching of Glass

Particularly used in the identification of the artist or factory on cut glass items, a stamp of the name to be etched is dipped in hydrofluoric acid, then applied to the glass where the acid eats away enough glass to leave the desired frosted mark.

Glass Cutting

After cooling and annealing, a design usually in ink, is sketched on the part by the "rougher" who cuts the broad outline of the design. Given then to the cutter who uses a copper, diamond, or silicon carbide wheel to refine the design. Both of these artisans are highly skilled, for an error scraps the piece.

Then it goes to the polisher who may skillfully finish the glass by using objects made of cork, poplar or willow wood, or by immersing in an acid bath.

Marks

Identification marks on knife rests may take several forms. Silver, properly hallmarked*, as discussed elsewhere in this book, is perhaps the easiest to identify. The Unites States Congress, in 1891, passed a law requiring any foreign merchandise sold in this country to carry information on its country of origin, including all rests made of metal, glass, or ceramics. This identification had been in the form of paper stickers, raised or impressed letters or backstamps. However, articles made for domestic sale need not and were not always so identified.

In the case of ceramics, most paper stickers, if there had been any, are long gone but fortunately, better potters used one or both of the other forms of marking: backstamps or the name impressed in the soft clay before firing. Dating from these marks can be readily verified. Metal knife rests frequently carry the factory names in raised or recessed letters along with other information.

Silver items were often sent long distances in England for hallmarking in London because of the prejudices against regional manufacturers and for the benefits a London hallmark would bring.

It has been pointed out that there is a similarity of logos, identification and factory marks, found on both thimbles and knife rests, especially metal. Yes, ceramic as well, for fine ceramic thimbles were made which command high prices today. Thimbles are still being manufactured for the souvenir trade.

The above should provide grist for study by collectors of either or both of these charming collectibles. The following publications could well be helpful. These books carry many pages of marks and logos identified with dates and manufacturers.

American Silver Thimbles by Gay Ann Rogers, 1989

Antique Sewing Tools and Tales by Barbara D. Gallers, 1992

Encyclopedia of American Silver Manufacturers by Dorothy Rainwater, 1975

Thimble Collectors Encyclopedia, New International Edition by John J. VanHoelle, 1986

Zalkins Handbook of Thimbles and Sewing Implements by Estelle Zalkins, 1988

*There are many books and booklets showing all the English and Irish hallmarks, their dates and locations where assayed. <u>Discovering Hallmarks on English Silver</u>, by John Bly, 1984, discusses and illustrates hallmarking. Bradbury's <u>Book of Hallmarks</u>, 1978, is also very good.

International Hallmarks on Silver by Tardy Paris, 1985 - An excellent reference, especially on European hallmarking.

British Registry Marks

This is a list of Registration Marks issued by the British Public Record Office. If you have any knife rests, or other art objects with the mark "Rd." followed by a number, using this chart, you will be able to find the year in which it was first registered.

	351202 = 1900	673750 = 1920
	368154 = 1901	680147 = 1921
	385180 = 1902	687144 = 1922
	403200 = 1903	696999 = 1923
1 = 1884	424400 = 1904	702671 = 1924
19754 = 1885	447800 = 1905	710165 = 1925
40480 = 1886	471860 = 1906	718057 = 1926
64520 = 1887	493900 = 1907	726330 = 1927
90483 = 1888	518640 = 1908	734370 = 1928
116648 = 1889	535170 = 1909	742725 = 1929
141273 = 1890	552000 = 1910	751160 = 1930
163767 = 1891	574817 = 1911	760853 = 1931
185713 = 1892	594195 = 1912	769670 = 1932
205240 = 1893	612431 = 1913	779292 = 1933
224720 = 1894	630190 = 1914	789019 = 1934
246975 = 1895	644935 = 1915	799097 = 1935
268392 = 1896	653521 = 1916	808794 = 1936
291241 = 1897	658988 = 1917	817293 = 1937
311658 = 1898	662872 = 1918	825231 = 1938
331707 = 1899	666128 = 1919	832610 = 1939

837520 = 1940	895000 = 1960	993012 = 1980
838590 = 1941	899914 = 1961	998302 = 1981
839230 = 1942	904638 = 1962	1004456 = 1982
839980 = 1943	909364 = 1963	1010583 = 1983
841040 = 1944	914536 = 1964	1017131 = 1984
842670 = 1945	919607 = 1965	1024174 = 1985
845550 = 1946	924510 = 1966	1031358 = 1986
849730 = 1947	929335 = 1967	1039055 = 1987
853260 = 1948	934515 = 1968	1047799 = 1988
856999 = 1949	939875 = 1969	1056078 = 1989
860854 = 1950	944932 = 1970	2003720 = 1990
863970 = 1951	950046 = 1971	2012047 = 1991
866280 = 1952	955342 = 1972	
869300 = 1953	960708 = 1973	
872531 = 1954	965185 = 1974	
876067 = 1955	969249 = 1975	
897282 = 1956	973838 = 1976	
882949 = 1957	978426 = 1977	
887079 = 1958	982815 = 1978	
891665 = 1959	987910 = 1979	

Illustrations

The beautiful illustrations of glass, ceramic, metal and other knife rests that follow would not have been possible without the contributions of these fine folks. I thank you for your generosity.

Christopher Bashford - Calgary, Alberta, Canada

Birmingham Museum of Art, Birmingham, Alabama

Brooklyn Museum of Art, Brooklyn, New York

William R. Donalson - Tallahassee, Florida

Anne Fairfield - Nashville, Tennessee

Jack Halpern - San Francisco, California

Don and Doreen Hornsblow - Braughing, England

T. H. Jacoway - Palatka, Florida

Richard Jefferson - Webster, New York

University of Leeds - Leeds, England

Richard and Joan Randles - Webster, New York

Dean L. Rockwell - Ypsilanti, Michigan

Barbara Ruby - Uniontown, Pennsylvania

John Simmons - Hartford, Connecticut

Victoria and Albert Museum - London, England

Paul Wakem - Webster, New York

The Wedgwood Museum - Barlaston, England

The Henry Francis DuPont Museum - Winterthur, Maryland

Glass Knife Rests

An excellent pressed glass *Cambridge* rest, from the Donalson collection.

A *Gillander* rest on the left, one by *Hoare* on the right, from the Donalson collection.

Unless otherwise specified, dimensions are in length only.

An array of fine cut crystal, from the Donalson collection.

A selection of fine cut crystal knife rests and related items, from the Donalson collection.

Unless otherwise specified, dimensions are in length only.

A multifaceted cut glass 4" signed
MACMILLAN in raised letters, from the Canadian factory.
Jefferson-Wakem collection.

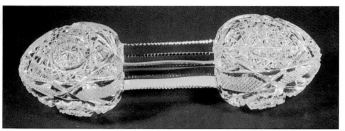

Brilliant Period cut glass crystal, "Creswick" pattern, signed *EGGLINTON*. Tear drops in each end connected through the crosspiece. 3 3/4" Jefferson-Wakem collection.

Brilliant Period cut crystal signed *EGGLINTON*. Ends lapidary cut 4 1/4". Jefferson-Wakem collection.

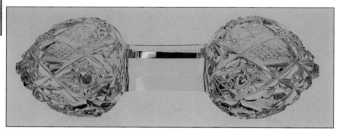

Brilliant Period cut crystal attributed to *HAWKES*. "Brazilian" pattern. Almond shape ends. 5 3/8". Jefferson-Wakem collection.

American cut crystal. Unusual fancy notched cut pattern, probably *BERGEN*. 5 5/8". Jefferson Wakem collection.

Brilliant cut crystal "Harvard" pattern. Probably *LIBBEY*. 5 3/4". Jefferson-Wakem collection.

Unless otherwise specified, dimensions are in length only.

Glass Knife Rests

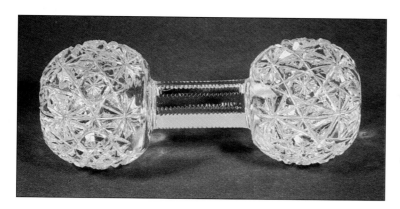

Cut crystal knife rest of the Brilliant Period. "Russian" pattern. Done by several glass cutting firms. Jefferson-Wakem collection.

Superb cut crystal probably *BERGEN*. "Dauntless" pattern. 4 1/2". From the Jefferson-Wakem collection.

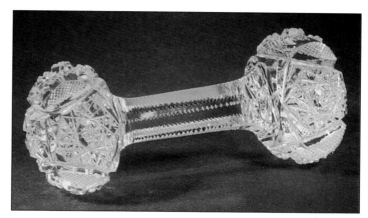

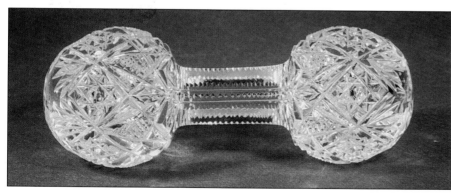

American cut crystal possibly by *DORFLINGER* or *HAWKES*. "Gladys" pattern, 4 1/4". Jefferson-Wakem collection.

Another cut crystal rest in the "Oval and Split" pattern attributed to *DORFLINGER*. 5 1/8". Jefferson-Wakem collection.

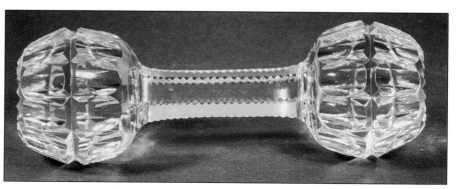

Unless otherwise specified, dimensions are in length only.

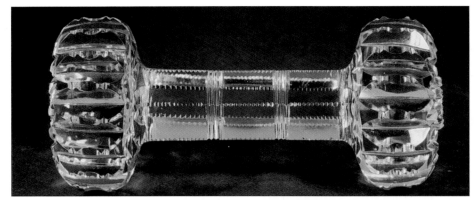

American brilliant crystal superbly cut with 16 point "hobstar" on its cylindrical ends 4 1/2" x 2 1/4". Jefferson-Wakem collection.

Bow tie cut crystal with raised diamond swirls. 4". Jefferson-Wakem collection.

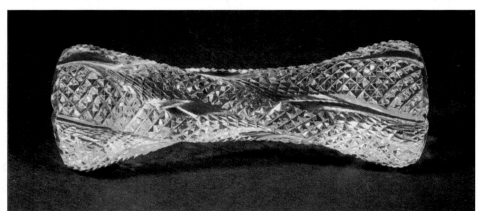

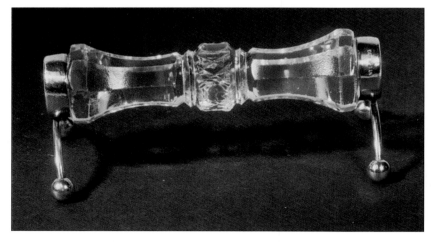

Cut glass and silver. Note "sterling" mark which likely makes it of American manufacture. 3 1/8" Jefferson-Wakem collection.

Cut, cross hatched, glass and English sterling silver. 3 7/8". Hallmark for Birmingham 1918, *L & S Silversmiths*. Jefferson-Wakem collection.

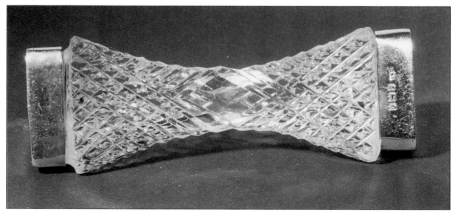

Unless otherwise specified, dimensions are in length only.

Libbey - Libbey began as the *New England Glass Company* in South Boston, Massachusetts, in 1818. The company went through several changes of ownership before being acquired by William Libbey in 1878. In 1888, Edward Drummond Libbey, who had become the owner of the firm on the death of his father, moved the factory to Toledo, Ohio, to take advantage of good railroads, cheaper labor, a deposit of high grade sandstone (silica) and a newly discovered pool of natural gas which was to provide the badly needed energy for making glass. Note the acid etched mark on this fine lapidary cut knife rest. 5 1/2", c. 1906. Rockwell collection

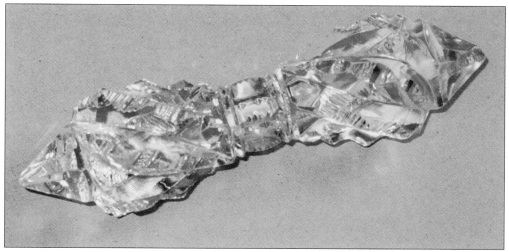

Unique shaped cut crystal. 5". Anne Fairfield collection.

Unless otherwise specified, dimensions are in length only.

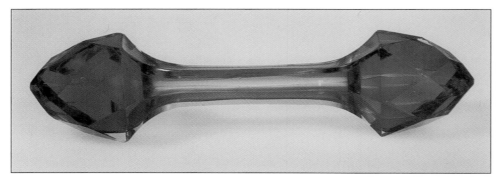

Exceptional
ruby cut glass.
Probably English.
4 1/2"
Randles collection.

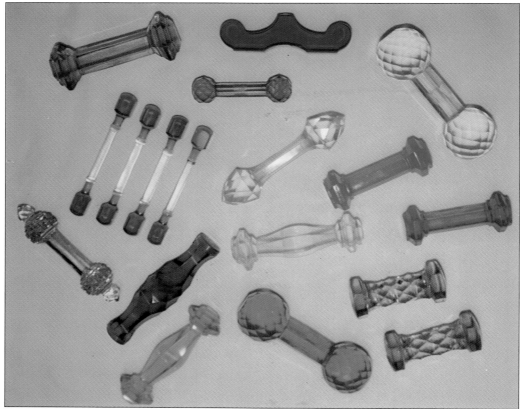

An attractive collage of colored glass. Jacoway collection.

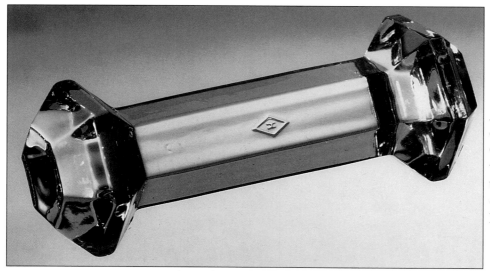

Heisey Glass Company established in Newark, Ohio in 1895. Its molds were purchased by the *Imperial Glass Company* in 1958. Rockwell collection.

Unless otherwise specified, dimensions are in length only.

John Hoare was born in Cork, Ireland, where he learned the glass cutting trade under his father. He immigrated to Philadelphia in 1853. In 1856. he and five partners formed a cutting shop. After many changes and different locations over the next twenty years, the company finally located in Corning, New York, as *J. Hoare and Company*. Most of their blanks came from the *Corning Glass Company* in New York. Collectors should note that knife rests or pieces that show the etched date of 1853 should not be misled. That is the date John Hoare came to the United States and formed his first business. 5 1/5". Rockwell collection.

Double, cut crystal knife rests, c. 1850. Rockwell collection

Unless otherwise specified, dimensions are in length only.

Ceramic Knife Rests

English pearlware, transfer printed in underglaze blue. Early 19th century. Impressed *Leeds Pottery* from the University of Leeds collection.

Possibly late 19th century French. Hand decorated. 3 1/2", Rockwell collection

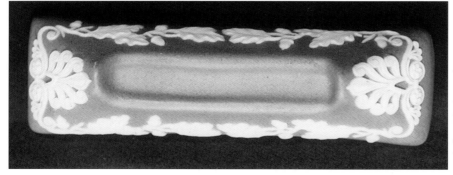

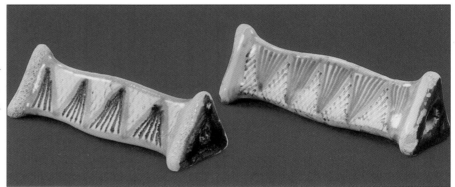

Pottery knife rest in imitation Wedgwood. Probably made by the *Ecanada Art Pottery Company*, Hamilton, Ontario, Canada. c. 1950. Note recess to catch the gravy. 4 1/2" - Halpern collection

Davenport, Staffordshire, England. An early 19th century family of potters well-known for their excellent blue printed ware. Name is usually backstamped in upper case letters. Rockwell collection.

Unless otherwise specified, dimensions are in length only.

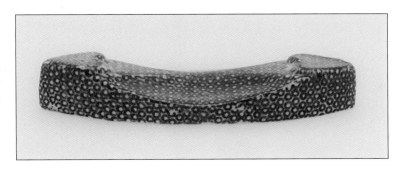

Meir, another 19th century Staffordshire, England manufacturer of transfer printed earthenware. Name is usually impressed. Rockwell collection.

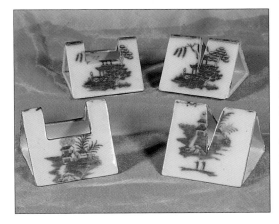

Swansea, Wales, England. These rests are probably from the *Glamorgan* factory formed in 1813, closed in 1839. Excellent body with good transfer printed decoration. Rockwell collection.

Two early earthenware knife rests, probably late 18th century, English creamware. This dating pushes back the appearance of this ware as knife rests. Rockwell collection.

Paul Bunyan - a mythic woodsman's hero of monstrous size and prodigious strength. A 9" knife rest from his estate. Rockwell collection.

Unless otherwise specified, dimensions are in length only.

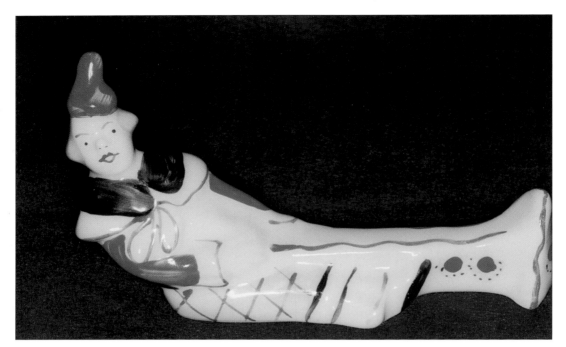

Clown, Russian, signed. Barbara Ruby collection.

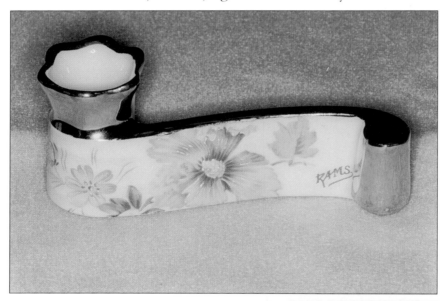

Knife rest with flower
holder. Signed *RAMS*
4" x 1 3/4".
Probably *Limoges*.
Barbara Ruby collection.

Attributed to German
manufacture. 1920.
3 1/8" x 1 3/8".
Barbara Ruby collection.

Unless otherwise specified, dimensions are in length only.

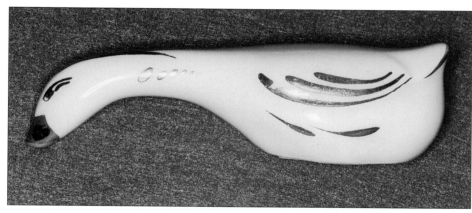

Signed *"Limoges, France"*.
4"
Barbara Ruby collection.

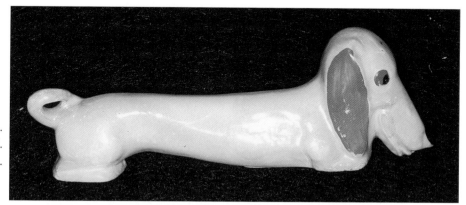

German or French.
Incised 1887.
Barbara Ruby collection.

Probably French.
c. 1950.
Barbara Ruby
collection.

This knife rest may very
likely be walrus ivory.
2 1/2" x 1 1/2".
Barbara Ruby collection.

Unless otherwise specified, dimensions are in length only.

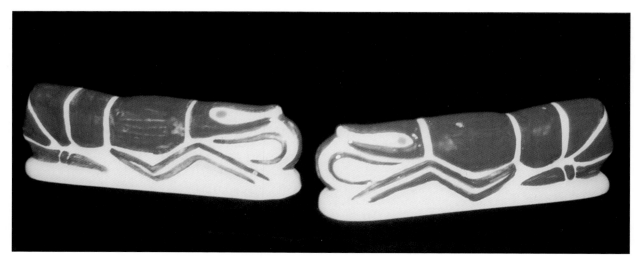

Earthenware lobsters. French, *Quimper*, pre WW II, 3". Hornsblow collection.

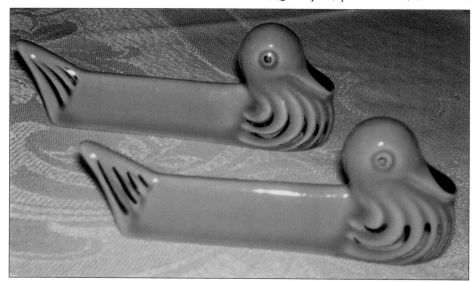

Probably French, pre WW II, 2 3/4". Hornsblow collection.

Appealingly designed and handpainted. French earthenware, pre WW II, 2 1/2". Hornsblow collection.

Unless otherwise specified, dimensions are in length only.

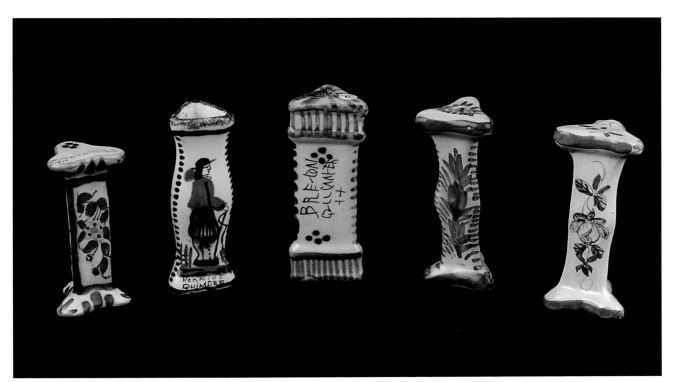

Early 20th century, French faience produced by from left to right; *Varengarille*, *Quimper*, *Quimper*, *Quimper*, and *Cancale*.
Rockwell collection

Sketches of *Wedgwood*. English, late 18th or early 19th century creamware. Each rest approximately 2 1/2".
Illustrated in the *1802 Drawing Book*.
By the courtesy of the Wedgwood Museum, Barlaston, Stoke-on-Kent, Staffordshire, England.

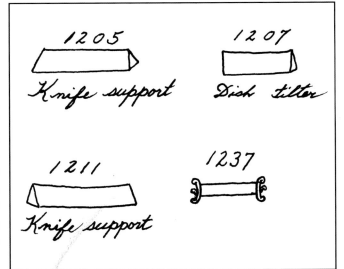

1205
Knife support

1207
Dish tilter

1211
Knife support

1237

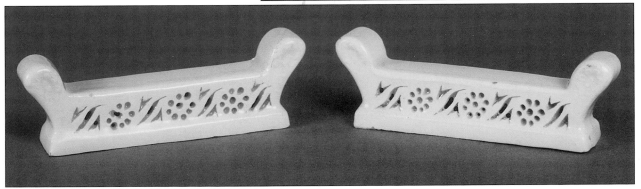

Creamware - ascribed to Italian manufacture, c. 1825. 3". Courtesy of the Victoria and Albert Museum, London, England.

Unless otherwise specified, dimensions are in length only.

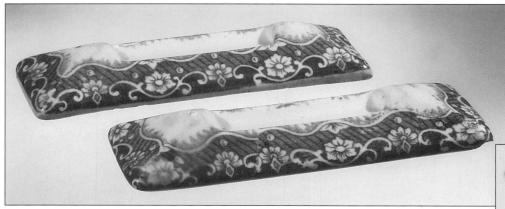

Spode, founded in 1776. Famed for its hand decorated porcelain and blue transfer printed earthenware. Knife rests with blue printed decorations were a staple of its production for at least the first 50 years of the 19th century. This pair carries both the backstamped and impressed *SPODE* name. Note the center trough to catch any gravy running down the carving knife or fork. 3 7/8". Rockwell collection.

Earthenware, tin enamel glaze, 3 5/8" x 1 5/8". Probably French, dated 1720-1760 as per letter of October, 1978. Courtesy of the Henry Francis duPont Winterthur Museum, Winterthur, Delaware.

Pottery knife rests with the universal willow decoration from an unknown manufacturer. 4 1/4". Rockwell collection.

Unless otherwise specified, dimensions are in length only.

Metal Knife Rests

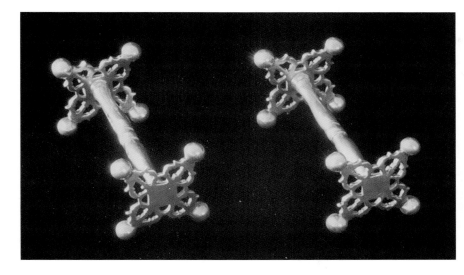

English silver, hallmark
1836 by William Bateman,
grandson of the
acclaimed silversmith,
Hester Bateman.
Rockwell collection.

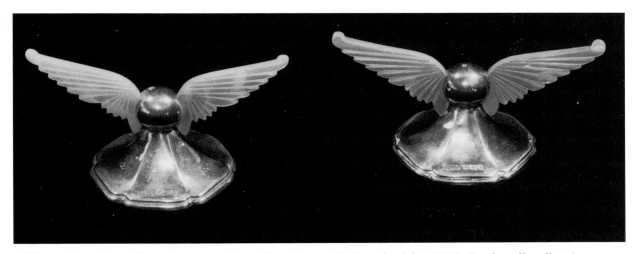

Wings of mother-of-pearl mounted on silver bases. Hallmarked for 1898. Rockwell collection.

An unusual
double knife rest,
9" long, most likely
for the carving
knife and fork.
Halpern
collection.

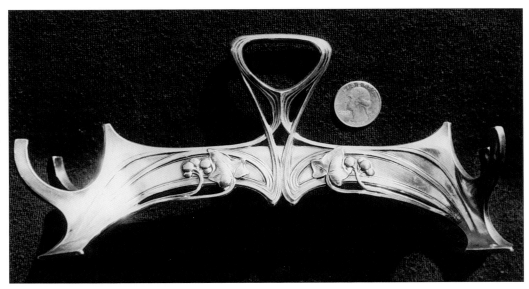

Unless otherwise specified, dimensions are in length only.

A combination rest, salt and flower vase. Probably 20th century, French. Halpern collection.

Unusual holder for horn handled carving set. 12" long. Simmons collection.

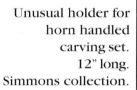

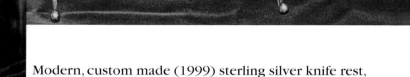

Modern, custom made (1999) sterling silver knife rest, impressed 925. 5 1/2" l x 2 1/2" h. Simmons collection.

Boxed set of silver plated and hardstone knife rests. Simmons collection.

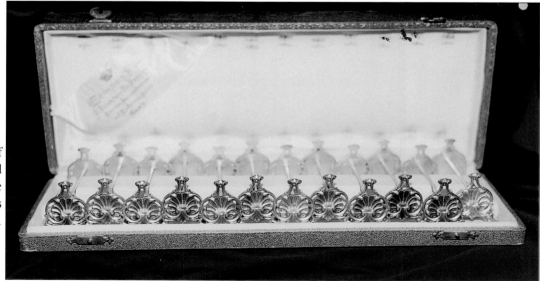

Unless otherwise specified, dimensions are in length only.

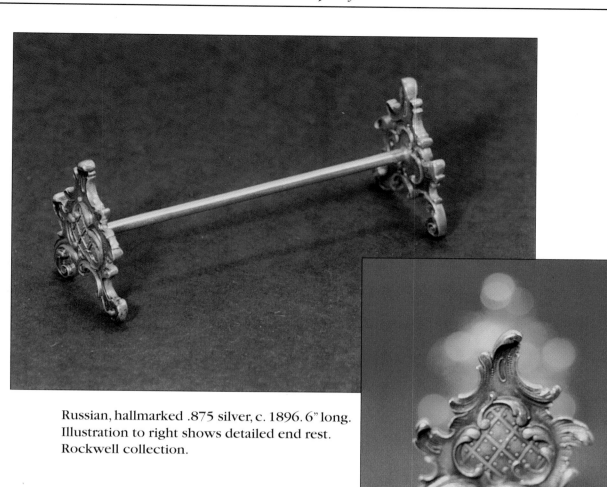

Russian, hallmarked .875 silver, c. 1896. 6" long.
Illustration to right shows detailed end rest.
Rockwell collection.

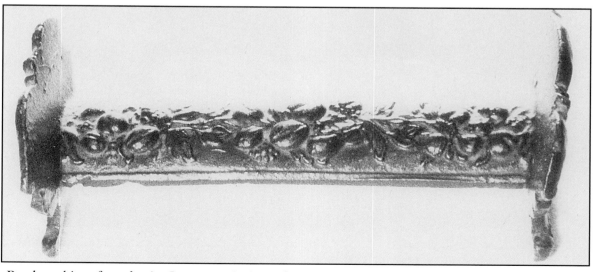

Produced in a foundry in Germany. Artist unknown, 8 cm long. Part of the 920 pieces of cast iron lent to the Birmingham Museum of Art, Birmingham, Alabama, by the *American Cast Iron Pipe Company*. Part of the Lamprecht collection.

Unless otherwise specified, dimensions are in length only.

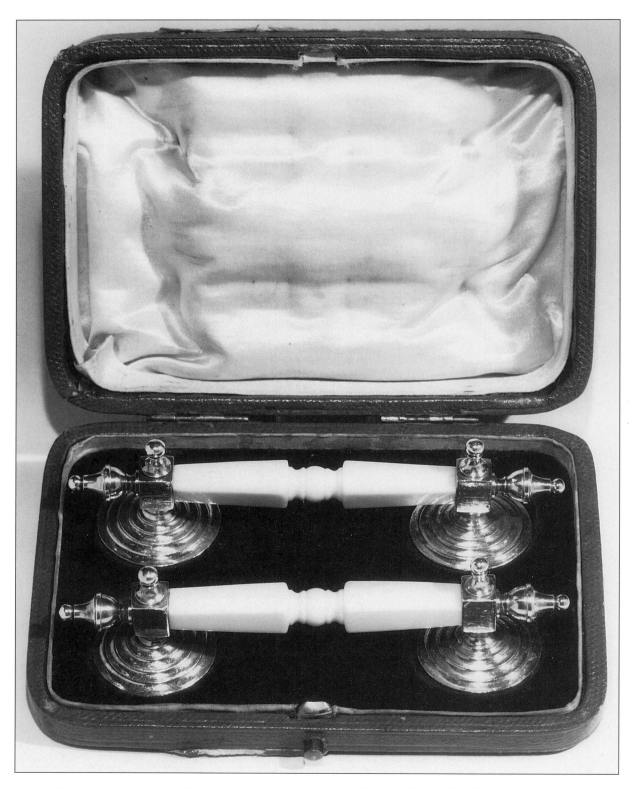

Boxed set of a pair of ivory and silver knife rests. Hallmarked 1886. Rockwell collection.

Unless otherwise specified, dimensions are in length only.

Other Knife Rests and Serving Pieces

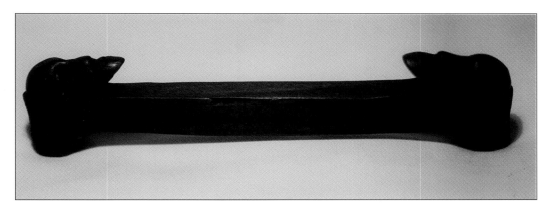

A carved African ebony wood knife rest. Halpern collection.

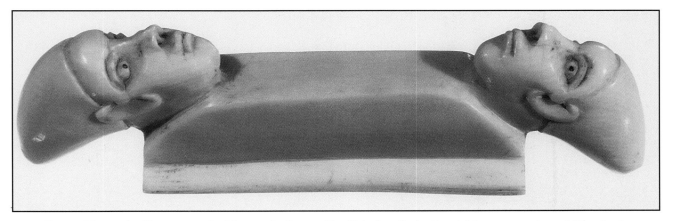

Carved ivory knife rest probably made for an English family in the African country of Rhodesia (now Zimbabwe). Late 19th century, 3 1/4". Rockwell collection.

Carving knife, fork and steel plus a fish knife and fork. The knife rests are of ivory with sterling mountings. Rockwell collection.

Unless otherwise specified, dimensions are in length only.

Trademarks and labels for American, Brilliant Period Cut Glass Wares, compliments of Louise Boggess, 1978.

J. D. Bergen Company
Meriden, Conn.

T. B. Clark & Company
Honesdale, Pa.

Libby Glass Company
Toledo, Ohio

Apr. 21, 1896

June 19, 1906

Apr. 16, 1901
(for use on pressed
[figured] blanks)

  Maple City Glass Co.
Honesdale, Pa.

Meriden Cut Glass Company
Meriden, Conn.

  Mt. Washington Glass Company
(Pairpoint Corporation)
New Bedford, Mass.

 Cut Glass Corporation of America
(Quaker City Cut Glass Co.)
Philadelphia, Pa.

C. Dorflinger & Sons
White Mills, Pa.

O. F. Egginton Company
Corning, N.Y.

  Empire Cut Glass Company
New York, N.Y.
Flemington, N.J.

TUTHILL CUT GLASS COMPANY
Middletown, New York

H. C. Fry Glass Co.
Rochester, Pa.

  T. G. Hawkes & Company
Corning, N.Y.

A. H. Heisey & Co., Inc.
Newark, Ohio   PLUNGER

CUT

MAPLE CITY GLASS COMPANY
Hawley, Pennsylvania

J. Hoare & Company
Corning, N.Y.

PAIRPOINT CORPORATION
New Bedford, Massachusetts

Imperial Glass Co.
Bellaire, Ohio

T. G. HAWKES & COMPANY
Corning, New York

PITKIN & BROOKS
Chicago, Illinois

J. HOARE & COMPANY
Corning, New York

H. P. SINCLAIRE & COMPANY

BIBLIOGRAPHY

American Cut and Engraved Glass by Albert Christian Revi, 1965

American Cut and Engraved Glass In Historical Perspective by Martha Louise Savan, 1986

American Cut Glass for the Discriminating Collector by Michael and Dorothy Pearson, 1965

Hester Bateman, Queen of English Silversmiths by David S. Shine

A Book About the Table by John Audry Jefferson, 1875

The Book of Household Management by Mrs. Isabella Beeton, 1888

T. B. Clark Glass Company by American Cut Glass Association

Collecting Old Glass — English and Irish by J. H. Yoxall, 1912

Cristalleries Du Val Saint Lambert, Corning Museum of Glass
        by Norma P. H. Jenkins, Retired Head Librarian

Cut and Engraved Glass of the Brilliant Period — In Historical Perspective
        by Martha Louise Swan, 1986

Decorating Glass — Painting, Embossing, Engraving and Etching
        by Polly Rothenberg, 1977

Discovering Hallmarks on English Silver by John Bly, 1984

Dinner is Served by Gerald Brett

Domestic Recipe Book by Miss Catherine Beecher

Early Victorian England, by G. M. Young

Eggington's Celebrated Cut Glass by J. Michael Pearson, 1982

The English at Table (1700-1970) A Visual History of Eating by Hampstead Arts Council, London

English Glass for the Collectors (1660-1860) by G. Bernard Hughes

English Home Life by Christina Hale, 1947

Engraved Glass (1952-1958) by Lawrence Whistler

Engraving and Decorating Glass by Barbara Norman, 1972

Faiences De Longwy — Longwy, A Small Faience Manufacturer in Northeast France
        by Dominique Freyful, 1992

French Faience by Arthur Lane, 1970

French Faience — Fantasie et Populaire of the 19th and 20th Centuries by Millicent S. Mali, 1986

Georgian England by A. E. Richardson, 1931

The Glass Collector — A Guide to Old English Glass by Maciver Perceval

The Glass of Frederick Carder by Paul V. Gardner, 1971

T. G. Hawkes & Company by the American Cut Glass Association, 1979

J. Hoare & Company by the American Cut Glass Association,
        Catalog Committee, Taylor Abernathy, Chairman, 1997

J. Hoare & Company by the American Cut Glass Association - Roger Hampton, Chairman

The Kovel's Collectors Guide to American Pottery, 1974

The Ladies Guide to True Politeness and Perfect Manners or Miss Leslie's Behavior Book - Philadel-phia by T. B. Peterson & Brothers, 1864

Libbey Glass Company — Cut Glass, Thirteen catalogs in chronological order (1894-1920), 1996

Libbey Glass Company, Cut Glass, reprint of their 1890 catalog

Libbey Glass Since 1818 — Pictorial History and Collectors Guide by Carl U. Fauster, 1979

McDougall's Household Management — A Text Book for Senior Girls, London and Edinburgh, 1880

Nineteenth Century Glass — Its Genesis & Development by Albert Christian Revi, 1967

Old Danish Silver by Gudman Boesen

The Pairpoint Corporation by Robert Hampton

Paperweights and Other Glass Curiosities by E. M. Elville, 1954

The Pottery of South Wales by W. J. Grant Davidson

Quaker City Glass Company by American Cut Glass Association, 1995

The Rituals of Dinners — The Origins, Evolution, Eccentricities and Meaning of Table Manners by Margaret Visser, 1991

The Story of Cutlery by J. B. Himsworth

Tales of the Table by Barbara Norman

We May Live Without Poetry, Music and Art

We May Live Without Conscience and
Live Without Heart

We May Live Without Friends

We May Live Without Books

But You and Me, My Friends,

We Can't Live Without Cooks

Author Unknown